GENERIC ELECTRONIC CIRCUIT COMPONENTS PROJECTS HANDS ON

Basic Lie Detector,Short out and Switch Polarity Protection,Solenoid Driver,Piezoelectric Sensor,Square Wave Generator etc..,

Anbazhagan K

CONTENTS

ACKNOW-LEDG-MENTS

The writer might want to recognize the diligent work of the article group in assembling this book. He might likewise want to recognize the diligent work of the Raspberry Pi Foundation and the Arduino bunch for assembling items and networks that help to make the

Internet of Things increasingly open to the overall population. Yahoo for the democratization of innovation!

INTRO-DUCTION

The Internet of Things (IOT) is a perplexing idea comprised of numerous PCs and numerous correspondence ways. Some IOT gadgets are associated with the Internet and some are most certainly not. Some IOT gadgets structure swarms that convey among themselves. Some are intended for a solitary reason, while some are increasingly universally useful PCs. This book is intended to demonstrate to you the IOT from the back to front. By structure IOT gadgets, the per

user will comprehend the essential ideas and will almost certainly develop utilizing the rudiments to make his or her very own IOT applications. These included ventures will tell the per user the best way to assemble their very own IOT ventures and to develop the models appeared. The significance of Computer Security in IOT gadgets is additionally talked about and different systems for protecting the IOT from un-approved clients or programmers. The most significant takeaway from this book is in structure the tasks yourself.

1. SHORT OUT PROTECTION CIRCUIT

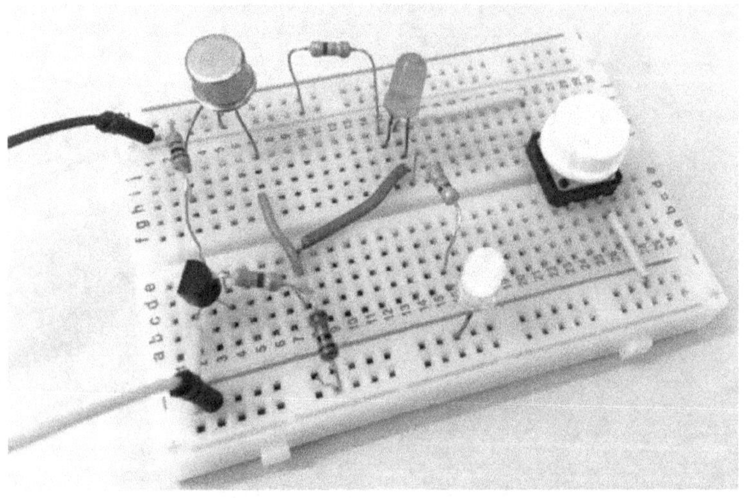

Short out is unintended association between two terminals which are providing capacity to the heap. It can happen both in AC or DC circuit, on the off chance that it is an AC supply, at that point short out can trip the force supply of entire zone, yet there are breakers and over-burden security circuits at numerous levels, from the force station to the house. What's more, in the event that it is a DC source like battery, at that point it can warm up the battery along with battery will be released rapidly. Now and again battery can be detonated. There are parcel of approaches to shield circuit from impede numerous kinds of breakers are accessible for over-burden assurance.

We are going to plan and study a basic low voltage Short-circuit insurance circuit for DC voltage. The circuit is structured with a reason to run microcontroller circuit securely and can shield it from harming because of short out in other piece of the hardware.

Segments required

- SK100B PNP transistor - 1Nos.

- BC547B NPN transistor - 1Nos.

- 1kω Resistor - 1Nos.

- 10kω Resistor - 1Nos.

- 330ω Resistor - 2Nos.

- 470ω Resistor - 1Nos.

- Force supply 6VDC - 1Nos.

- Breadboard - 1Nos.

- Associating wires - according to necessity

SK100B PNP Transistor

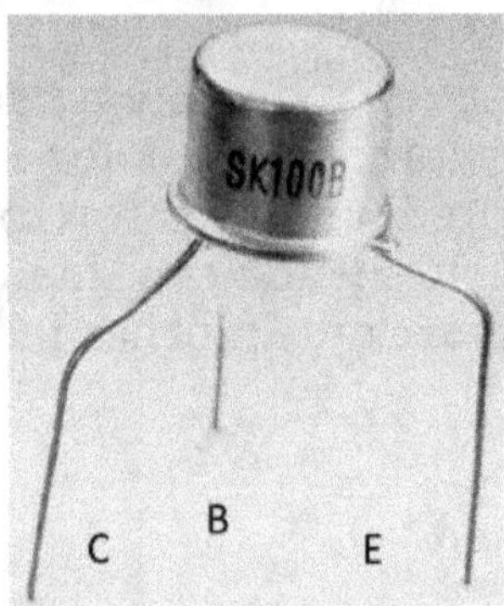

Beginning from the indent of the transistor is Emitter, center is base and last is Collector

- Producer - E

- Base - B

- Authority - C

BC547B NPN transistor

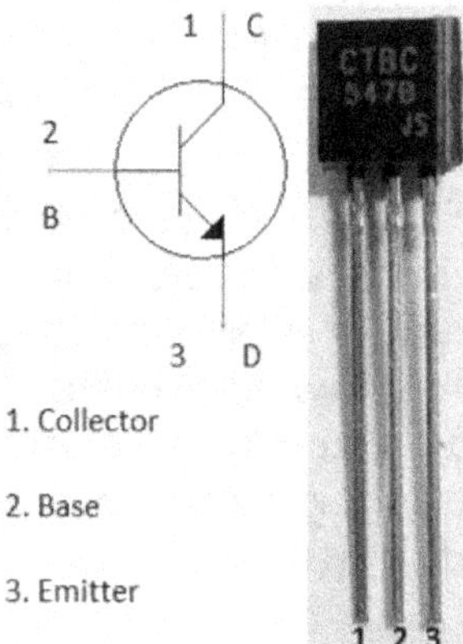

Short out Protection Circuit

A typical case of short out is when positive and negative terminal of a battery are associated together with a low-opposition conveyor, similar to a wire. In this condition, battery can set to fire and can even detonate. That is the thing that occurs with portable batteries in mobiles at ordinarily.

To keep away from this short out condition, Short-circuit Protection Circuit is utilized. Short out Protection Circuit will redirect the progression of current or break the contact between the circuit along with the force source.

Here and there we experience power disappointment with an unexpected flash while utilizing some flawed home apparatuses like broiler, iron, and so on, at that point. The purpose for this is, some place there is some overabundance current courses through some circuit inside that broken machine. This may prompt stun or could start up the house if not secured. So a wire or electrical switch is utilized so as to maintain a strategic distance from such harm. In such condition electrical switch or circuit disengages the fundamental inventory to the house. A wire breaker circuit is additionally a type of short out assurance circuit, in which a low opposition wire is utilized which melts and detaches the primary force supply to house at whatever point there is abundance current go through it.

So here we are going to study and configuration circuit to evade the harm because of short out in it.

Circuit Diagram

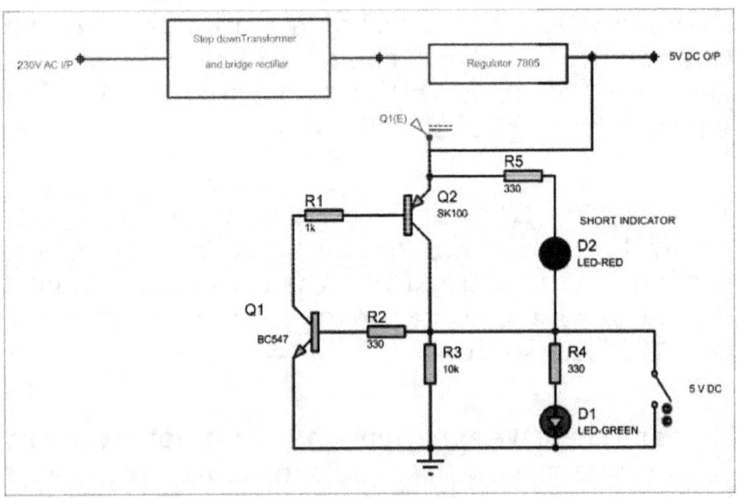

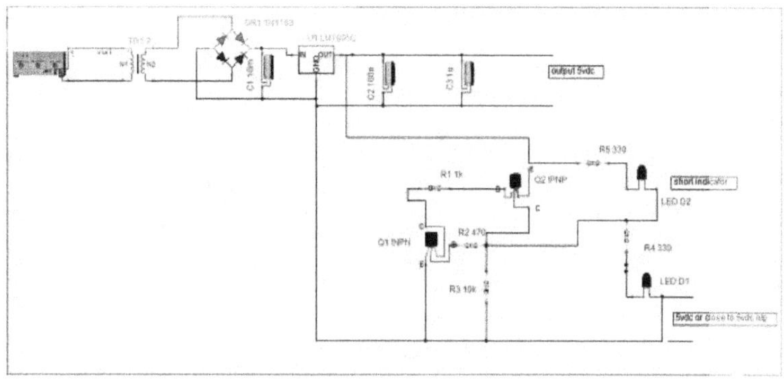

Working of Short Circuit Protection Circuit

A basic low force DC Short-circuit Protection Circuit is appeared above which comprises two transistor circuits, one is BC547 Negative Positive Negative transistor circuit along with other is SK100B Positive Negative Positive transistor circuit. The info is given to the circuit utilizing a 5V DC Power supply, which can be either given by some battery or utilizing transformer.

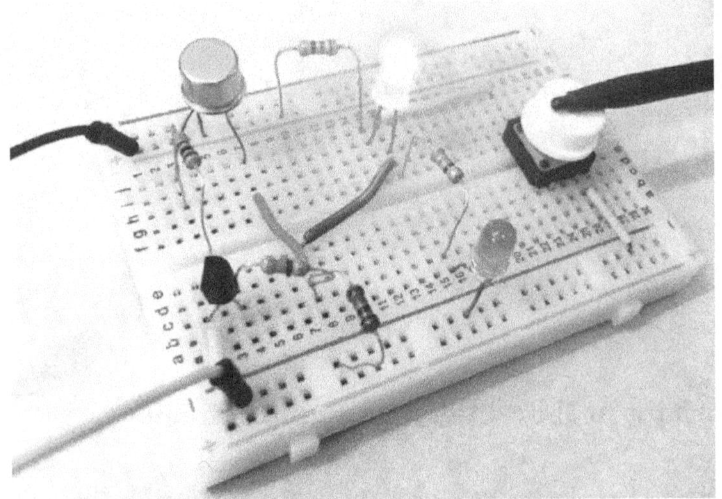

The working of the circuit is straightforward, when Green LED D1 gleams implies the circuit is working typically and there is no danger of harm. The Red LED D2 is needed to shine just when there is short out.

At the point when the force supply is turned ON, transistor Q1 gets one-sided and begins directing and LED D1 gets turns ON. During this time Red Light Emitting Diode D2 stays off as there is no Short-circuit.

The shining of Green LED D1 likewise shows that the stock voltage and yield voltage is roughly equivalent.

In our incitement circuit we have created a 'short' utilizing a switch at the yield. When the 'short' happens the yield voltage drops to 0V and Q1 quits directing as its base voltage is 0V. Transistor Q2 likewise quits leading as its authority voltage additionally dropped to 0V.

So now current is begun moving through RED drove D2 and go through the ground by means of the short out way (through the switch). That makes Red LED D2 begins leading for what it's worth forward one-sided and shows that a short has been distinguished and the current is redirected through the RED Light Emitting Diode D2 as opposed to harming the whole circuit.

2. SWITCH POLARITY PROTECTION CIRCUIT

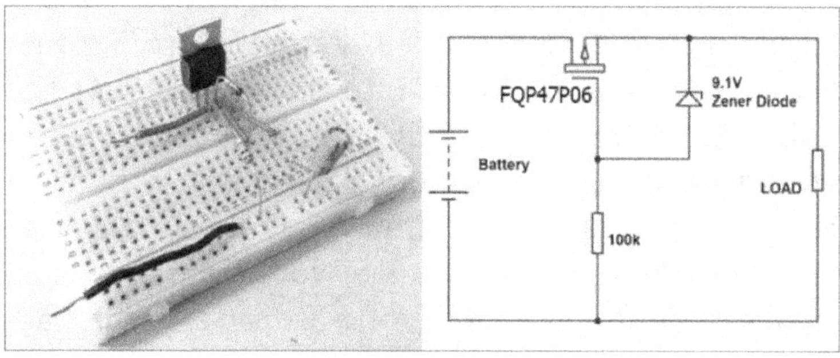

Batteries are most helpful force source to supply voltage to an electronic circuit. There are numerous many ways, to control up electronic gadgets, similar to connector, sun oriented cell and so forth however the most often recognized Direct Current power supply is Battery. By and large all the gadgets accompany Reverse Polarity Protection Circuit however on the off chance that you have any battery worked gadget which don't have invert extremity security then you generally must be cautious while changing the battery else it can explode the gadget.

In this way, in this circumstance Reverse Polarity Protection Circuit would be a valuable expansion to the circuit. There are few basic techniques to shield the circuit from turn around extremity association, for example, utilizing a diode otherwise Diode Bridge or by utilizing P-Channel MOSFET as a switch on HIGH side.

Turn around Polarity Protection utilizing Diode

Utilizing a Diode is the most straightforward and least expensive strategy for Reverse Polarity Protection yet it has an issue of intensity spillage. At the point when the info supply voltage is high a little voltage drop may regardless, particularly when the current is low. Be that as it may, if there should arise an occurrence of low voltage working framework, even a modest quantity of voltage drop is unsatisfactory.

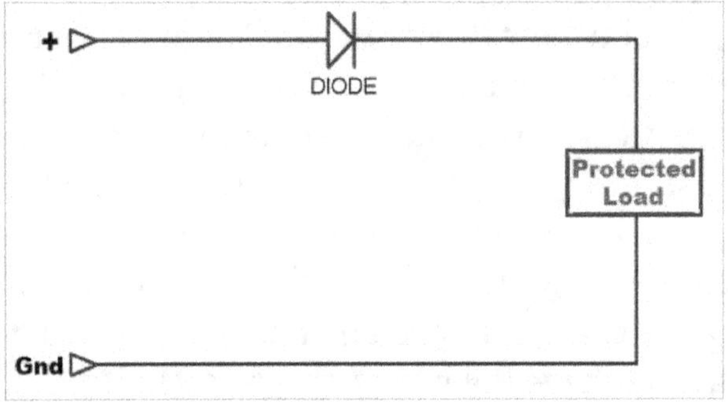

As we probably am aware the voltage drop over a universally useful diode is 0.7V so we can constrain this voltage drop by utilizing Schottky diode since its voltage drop is around 0.3V to 0.4V and it can likewise withstand with high current burdens. Know while picking a Schottky diode, since bunches of Schottky diodes accompanies high converse current spillage so ensure that you will pick one with low opposite current (under 100uA).

At four Amps, power misfortune by a Schottky diode in the circuit will be:

4 x 0.4W = 1.6W

Also, in standard diode:

4 x 0.7 = 2.8W.

You can even utilize a Full-connect rectifier for turn around extremity security, as it is paying little heed to extremity. In any case, connect rectifier comprises of four diodes, subsequently the measure of intensity waste will be twice of the force squander in the above circuit with single diode.

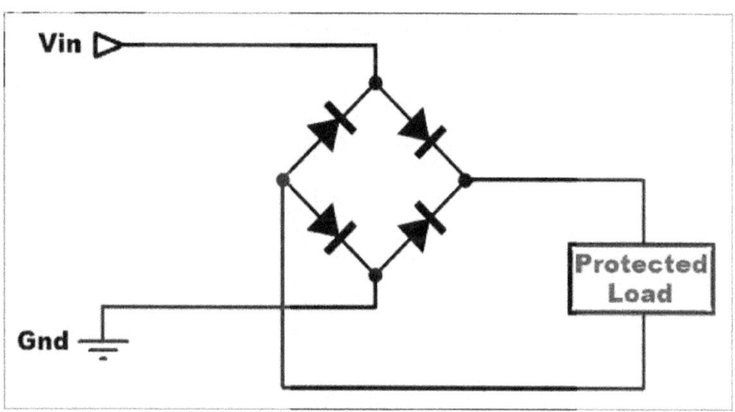

Switch Polarity Protection utilizing P-Channel MOSFET

Utilizing a P-Channel MOSFET for Reverse Polarity Protection is more dependable than different strategies, in light of low voltage drop as well as high current capacity. The circuit contains of a P-Channel MOSFET, Zener diode as well as a draw down resistor. In the event that the inventory voltage is not exactly the Gate-to-Source voltage (Vgs) of P-channel MOSFET then you just need the MOSFET without diode or resistor. You simply need to interface the entryway terminal of the MOSFET to the ground.

Presently, in case the stockpile voltage is more than the Vgs, in this point you require to drop the voltage between the door terminal and source. Parts required for making the circuit equipment is referenced underneath.

Material Required

- FQP47P06 P-Channel MOSFET

- Resistor (100k)

- 9.1V Zener Diode

- Breadboard

- Associating Wires

Circuit Diagram

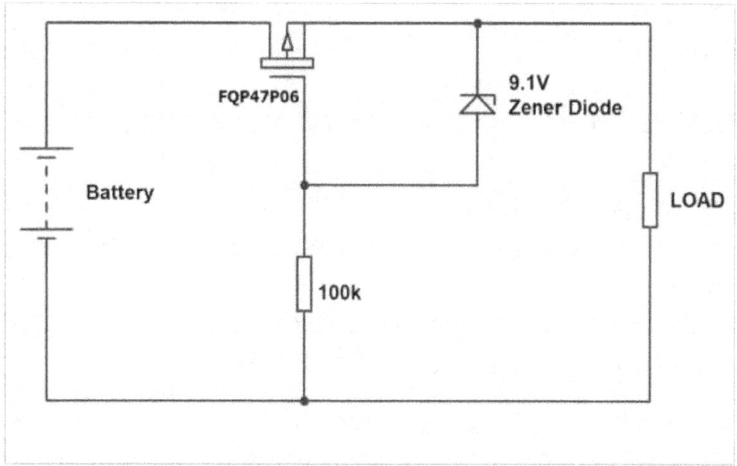

Working of Reverse Polarity Protection Circuit Using P-Channel MOSFET

Presently, when you associate the battery according to the circuit outline, with right extremity, it makes the transistor turn ON and permits the current to move through it. On the off chance that the battery is associated in reverse or in switch extremity, at that point the transistor kills and your circuit gets secured.

This insurance circuit is more proficient than others. How about we examine the circuit when the battery is associated in right manner, the P-Channel MOSFET will turn ON in light in case the voltage among entryway and source is negative. Recipe for finding the voltage among door and source is:

$$Vgs = (Vg - Vs)$$

In this point when the battery is associated erroneously, the voltage at door terminal will be sure and we realize that P-Channel MOSFET possibly turns on when the voltage at entryway terminal is negative (least - 2.0V for this MOSFET or less). So at whatever point battery is associated backward heading the circuit will be ensured by the MOSFET.

Presently, we should discuss the force misfortune in the circuit, when the transistor is ON the opposition among channel and source is practically unimportant yet to be progressively precise you can use the datasheet of the P-Procedure MOSFET. For FQP47P06 P-channel MOSFET the Static Drain-Source On-Resistance (RDS(ON)) is 0.026?(max.). In this way, we can figure the force misfortune in circuit like underneath:

$$Power\ Loss = I^2R$$

We should accept the present course through the transistor is 1A. So the force misfortune will be

$$\textbf{Power Loss} = I^2R = (1A)^{2}*0.026\Omega = 0.026W$$

Consequently, the force misfortune is around multiple times lesser than the circuit utilizing single diode. That is the reason utilizing a P-Channel MOSFET for Reverse Polarity Protection is much better than different strategies. It is tad costlier than diode however it makes the insurance circuit a lot more secure and effective.

We have likewise utilized a Zener Diode and a resistor in the circuit for the security against surpassing door to source voltage. By including the resistor and the Zener diode of 9.1V, we can brace the entryway source voltage to a limit of negative 9.1V, consequently the transistor stays safe.

3. PUSH-PULL AMPLIFIER CIRCUIT

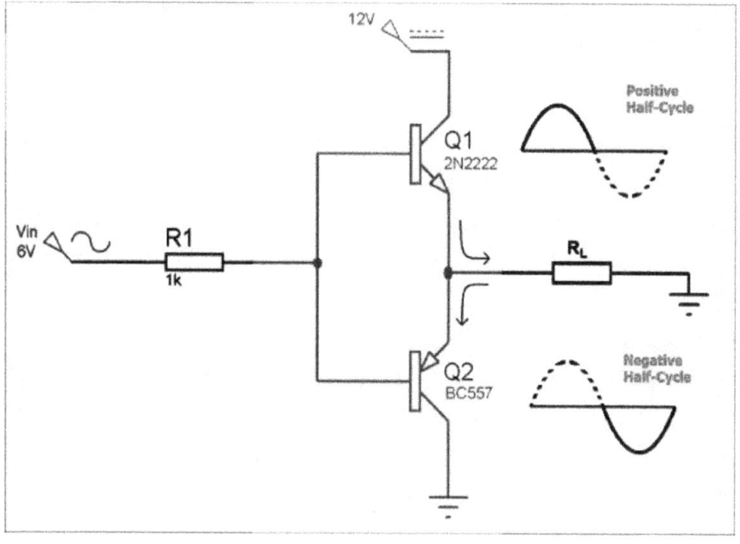

Push-Pull Amplifier is a force intensifier which is utilized to supply high capacity to the heap. It comprises of two transistors in which one is NPN and another is PNP. 1 transistor pushes the yield on +ve half cycle along with different pulls on -ve half cycle, this is the reason it is called as Push-Pull Amplifier. The upside of Push-Pull intensifier is that no way force scattered in yield transistor when sign is absent. There are three arrangement of Push-Pull Amplifier however for the most part Class B Amplifier is considered as Push Pull Amplifier.

- Class An intensifier

- Class B intensifier

- Class AB intensifier

Class An Amplifier

Class A design is the most widely recognized force speaker setup. It comprises of just one exchanging transistor which is set to stay ON consistently. It produces least twisting and greatest sufficiency of yield signal. The effectiveness of Class An strengthener is low close to 30%. The phases of the Class An enhancer permits same measure of burden current to move through it in any event, when there isn't input signal associated, subsequently enormous heatsinks are required for the yield transistors. The circuit graph for Class A speaker is given underneath:

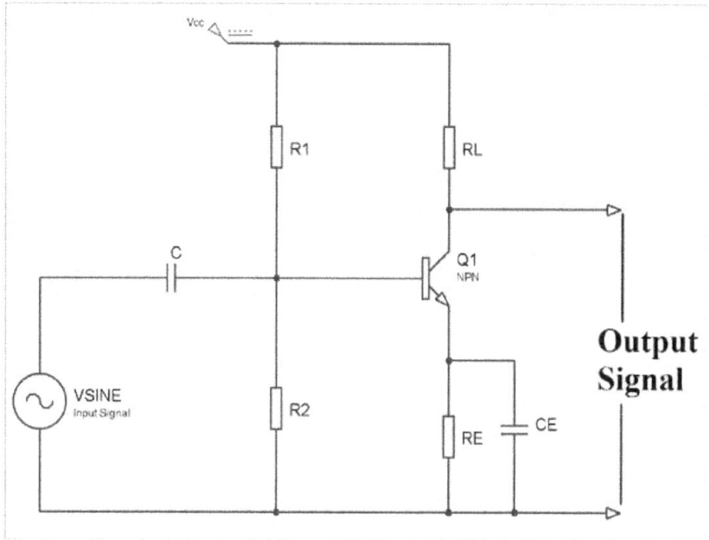

Class B Amplifier

Class B enhancer is the real Push-Pull Amplifier. Productivity of Class B speaker is > Class An intensifier, as it comprises of two transistors Negative Positive Negative along with Positive Negative Positive. The Class B enhancer circuit is one-sided so that every transistor will take a shot at one half pattern of the info waveform. In this way, the conduction edge of this sort of speaker circuit is 180 Degree. 1 transistor pushes the yield on +ve half cycle along with different pulls on -ve half cycle, this is the reason it is called as Push-Pull Amplifier. Circuit graph for Class B speaker is given beneath:

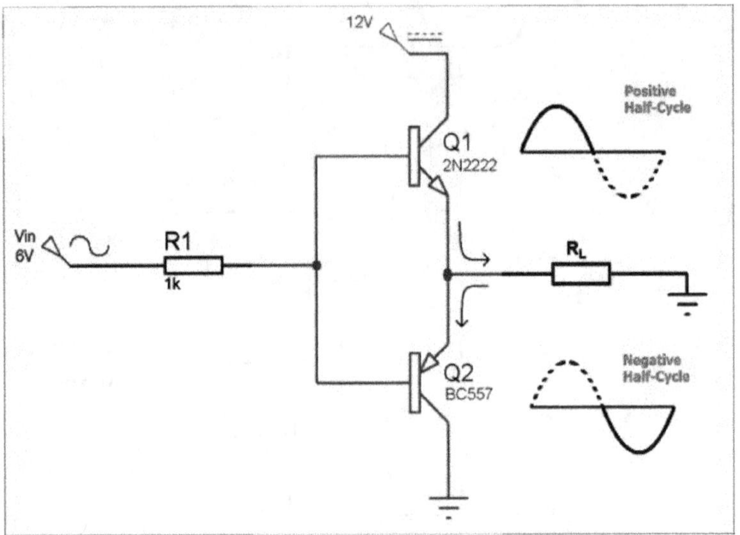

Class B for the most part experiences an impact known as Crossover Distortion in which sign get mutilated at 0V. We realize that, a transistor requires 0.7v at its base-producer intersection to turn it on. So when AC input voltage is given to push-pull speaker, it begins expanding from 0 and until it spans to 0.7v, transistor stays in OFF state along with we don't get any yield. Same thing occur with PNP transistor in negative half pattern of AC wave, this is called Dead Zone. To conquer this issue, diodes are utilized for biasing, and afterward the intensifier is known as Class AB Amplifier.

Class AB Amplifier

A typical technique to expel that hybrid mutilation in Class B speaker is to inclination both the transistor at a point somewhat above then the cut-off purpose of transistor. At that point this circuit is known as Class AB enhancer circuit. Hybrid contortion is later clarified in this article.

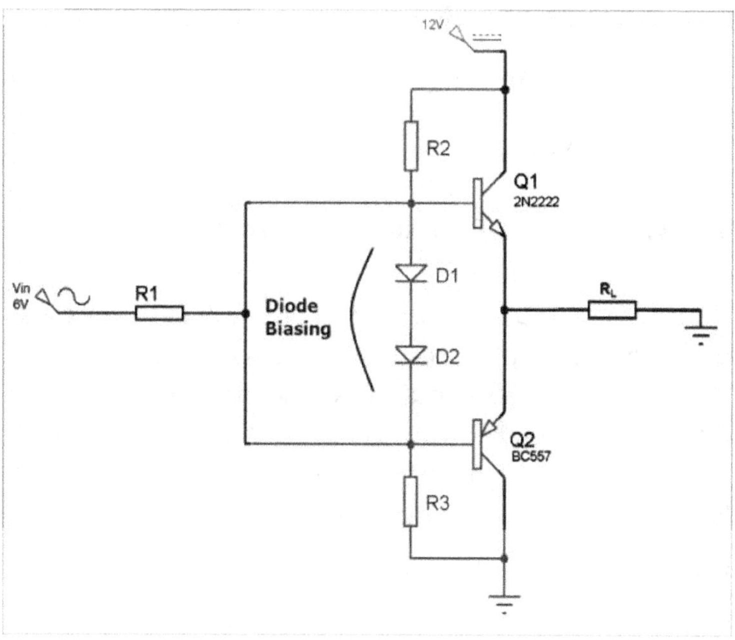

The Class AB speaker circuit is the mix of both Class An along with Class B enhancer. By including the diode, transistors are one-sided in somewhat directing state in any event, when no sign is available at base terminal, in this way evacuating the hybrid mutilation issue.

Materials Required

- Transformer (6-0-6)

- BC557-PNP Transistor

- 2N2222-NPN Transistor

- Resistor – 1k (2 nos)

- Driven

Working of Push-Pull Amplifier Circuit

The circuit graph for Push-Pull enhancer circuit comprises of two transistor Q1 along with Q2 which are NPN and PNP individually. At the point when the information signal is sure Q1 begins leading and produce a copy of the positive contribution at the yield. Right now Q2 stays in off condition.

Here, in this condition

$$V_{OUT} = V_{IN} - V_{BE1}$$

Likewise, when information signal is negative Q1 kills and Q2 begins directing and produce a reproduction of the negative contribution at the yield.

In this condition,

$$V_{OUT} = V_{IN} + V_{BE2}$$

Presently why the hybrid mutilation is going on when VIN compasses to zero? Let me give you harsh qualities outline and yield wave type of Push-Pull Amplifier Circuit.

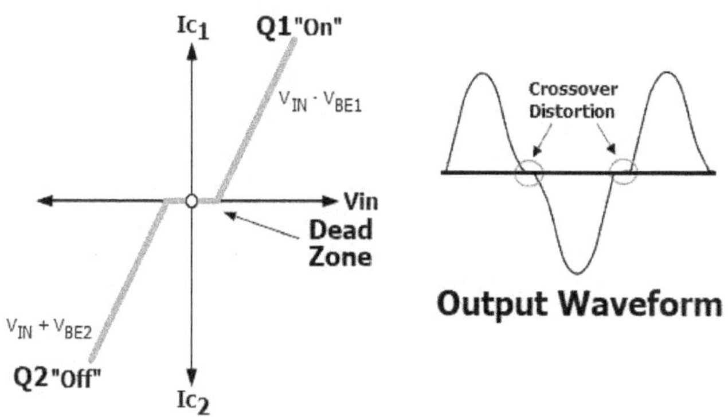

Transistor Q1 along with Q2 can't be all the while ON, for Q1 to be on we require that VIN must be more noteworthy than Vout and for Q2 Vin must be not exactly Vout. In case VIN is equivalent to zero, at that point Vout should likewise be equivalent to zero.

Presently when VIN is expanding from zero, the yield voltage Vout will stay zero until VIN is under VBE1 (which is approx. 0.7v), where VBE is the voltage needed to turn on the NPN transistor Q1. Thus, the yield voltage is showing a no man's land during the period VIN is not exactly VBE or 0.7v. This equivalent thing will happen when VIN is diminishing from zero, PNP transistor Q2 won't lead until the VIN is more noteworthy than VBE2 (~0.7v), where VBE2 is the voltage required to turn ON transistor Q2.

4. VOLTAGE REGULATOR CIRCUITS

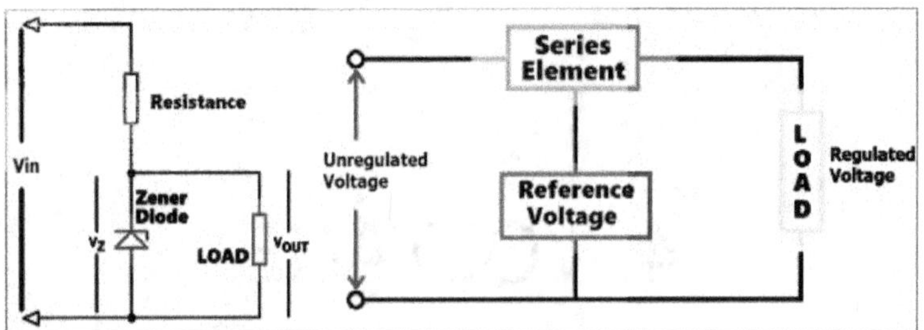

Voltage Regulator, as name recommends, is a circuit is utilized to control the voltage. Managed voltage is smooth inventory of voltage, liberated from any clamor or aggravation. The yield from voltage controller is autonomous of burden current, temperature and AC line variety. Voltage controllers are available in pretty much every gadgets or house hold apparatuses like TV, Fridge, PC and so on, to balance out the stockpile voltage.

Essentially, voltage controller limits the variety in voltage to ensure the gadget. In electrical circulation framework, the voltage controllers are either in feeder lines or at substation. There are 2 sorts of controllers utilized in this line, one is step controller, in which switches manage the present stock. Another is enlistment controller, which is a rotating electrical machine like an acceptance engine supplies power as an auxiliary source. It limits the voltage variety and give stable yield.

There are various sorts of voltage controllers which are clarified underneath.

Sorts of Voltage Regulator Circuit

Straight Voltage Regulator Circuit

- Arrangement Voltage Regulator

- Shunt Voltage Regulator

Zener Voltage Regulator Circuit

Exchanging Voltage Regulator Circuit

- Buck type

- Lift type

- Buck/Boost type

Straight Voltage Regulator Circuit

These are the most widely recognized controllers utilized in hardware to keep up the consistent yield voltage. Straight voltage controllers acts like a voltage divider circuit, in this controller opposition shifts concerning change in burden and gives consistent yield voltage. A few focal points and drawbacks of straight voltage controller are given underneath:

Preferences

- Yield swell voltage is low

- Reaction is quick

- Less commotion

Disservices

- Low effectiveness

- Huge space required

- Yield voltage will consistently be not as much as info voltage

1. Arrangement Voltage Regulator

Arrangement Voltage Regulator is a piece of Linear Voltage Regulator and furthermore called as Series Pass Regulator. A variable component associated in arrangement, utilized for keeping up consistent yield voltage. As you change the opposition of arrangement component voltage drop across it very well may be fluctuated to guarantee that the voltage across yield is consistent.

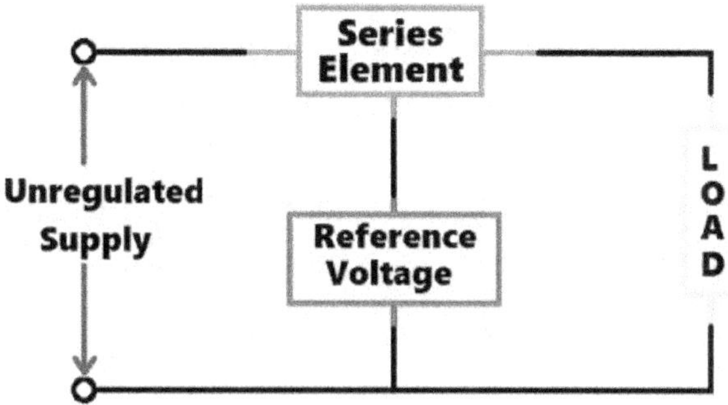

As should be obvious the circuit graph for Series Voltage Regulator, NPN transistor T1 is the arrangement component and a zener diode is utilized to give the reference voltage.

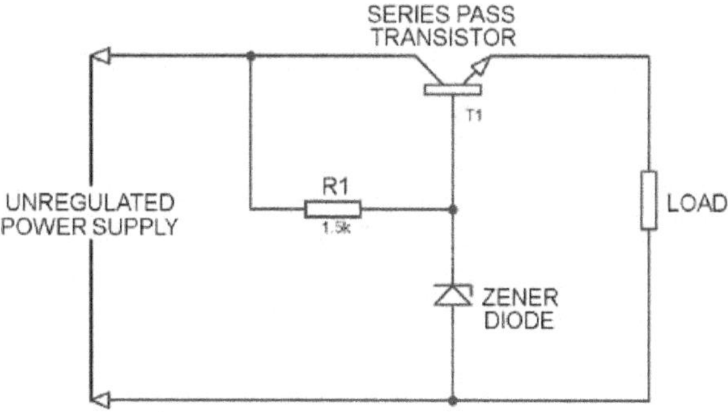

At the point when the yield voltage builds the base-producer voltage diminishes, because of this transistor T1 lead less. As T1 leads less it decrease the yield voltage henceforth keeps up the yield voltage consistent.

At the point when the yield voltage diminishes the base-producer voltage increments, because of this transistor T1 lead more. As T1 directs more it increment the yield voltage subsequently keeps up the yield voltage steady.

The yield voltage is characterized as:

$$V_O = V_Z - V_{BE}$$

Where,

V_O is the output voltage

V_Z is Zener breakdown voltage

V_{BE} is base-emitter voltage

2. Shunt Voltage Regulator

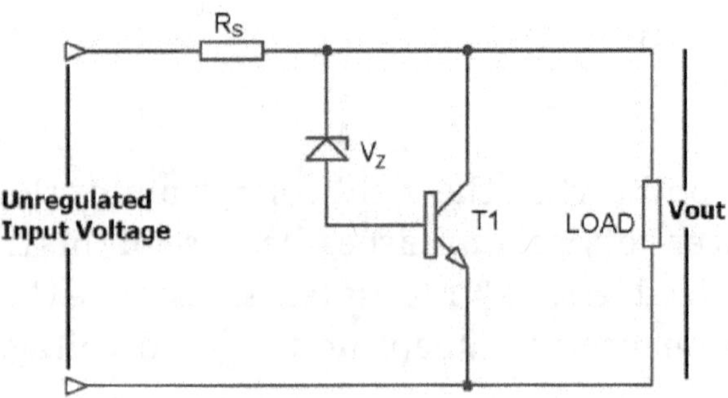

The unregulated voltage is straightforwardly corresponding to the voltage drop over the obstruction associated in arrangement and this voltage drop relies on the current devoured by the heap. In the event that the present utilization of burden builds the base current will likewise decrease and because of this less gatherer current will course through the authority producer terminal and henceforth the current through burden will increment and the other way around.

The controlled yield voltage of shunt voltage controller is characterized as:

$$V_{OUT} = V_Z + V_{BE}$$

Zener Voltage Regulator

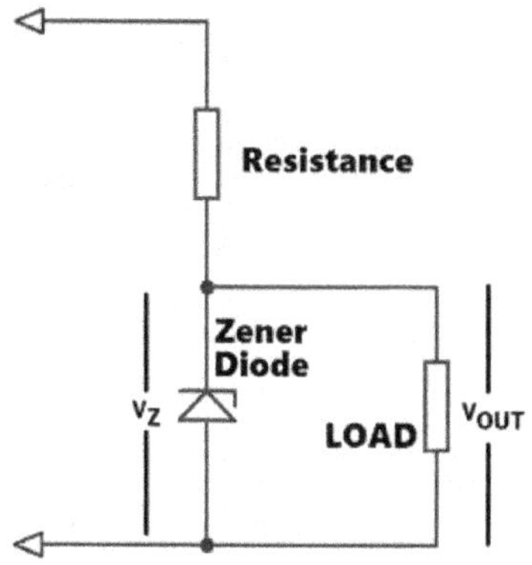

Zener Voltage Regulators are less expensive and just reasonable for low force circuits. It tends to be used in applications where the measure of intensity squandered during guideline isn't of significant concern.

A resistor, is associated in arrangement with the zener diode to restrain the measure of current moving across the diode along with the information voltage Vin (Which must be more prominent than the zener voltage) is associated across as appeared in the picture and the poduce voltage Vout, is taken over the zener diode with Vout = Vz (Zener Voltage). As we probably am aware Zener diode begins leading backward course when the given voltage is higher than the breakdown voltage of Zener. So when its beginning directing, it keeps up a similar voltage across it and stream back the additional current, accordingly give the steady yield voltage.

Get familiar with Zener Diode working here.

Exchanging Voltage Regulator

There are three sorts of exchanging voltage controller:

- Buck or Step-Down Switching Voltage Regulator

- Lift or Step-Up Switching Voltage Regulator

- Buck/Boost Switching Voltage Regulator

Buck or Step-Down Switching Voltage Regulator

A Buck Regulator is utilized to step down the voltage at the yield, we can even utilize the voltage divider circuit to decrease the yield voltage yet the productivity of voltage divider circuit is low, since resistors disperses vitality as warmth. We use capacitor, diode, inductor along with switch in the circuit. The circuit chart for Buck Switching Voltage Regulator is given beneath:

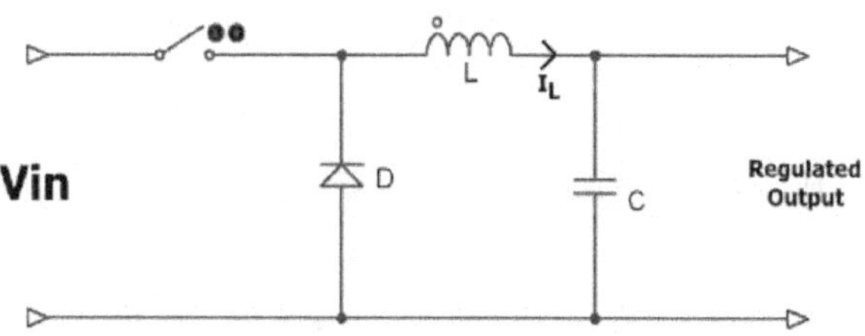

At the point when the switch in ON the diode stay turned around one-sided and power supply is combined with the inductor. At the point when the switch is open the extremity of inductor get opposite and the diode become forward one-sided and associate the inductor to the ground. At that point the current through the inductor diminishes with incline:

$$dI_L / dt = (0 - V_{OUT}) / L$$

The Capacitor is utilized to keep the voltage from dropping to zero over the heap. In case we continue opening and shutting switch the normal voltage over the heap will be not exactly the provided input voltage. You can control the produce voltage by changing the obligation pattern of the exchanging gadget.

Output Voltage = (Input Voltage) * (percentage of time that the switch is ON)

In case you need to become familiar with Buck converter than follow the connection.

Lift or Step-Up Switching Voltage Regulator

The Boost Regulator is utilized to step-up the voltage over the heap. The circuit graph for support controller is given beneath:

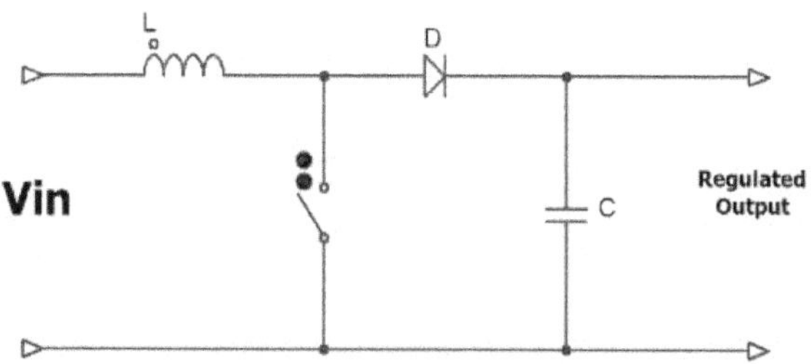

At the point when the switch is shut the diode acts as turned around one-sided and the current over the inductor continues expanding. Presently when the switch is opened, the inductor will make a power making the present keep streaming and capacitor begins charging. By constant killing the switch ON and we will get the voltage at the heap > the information voltage. We can manage the yield voltage by controlling the turn ON (Ton) time of the switch.

Output Voltage = Input Voltage / Percentage of time that the switch is open

In case you need to get familiar with Boost converter than follow the connection.

Buck-Boost Switching Voltage Regulator

Buck-Boost Switching Regulator is the blend of both Buck and Boost Regulator, it gives upset yield which can be more prominent or not exactly the provided input voltage.

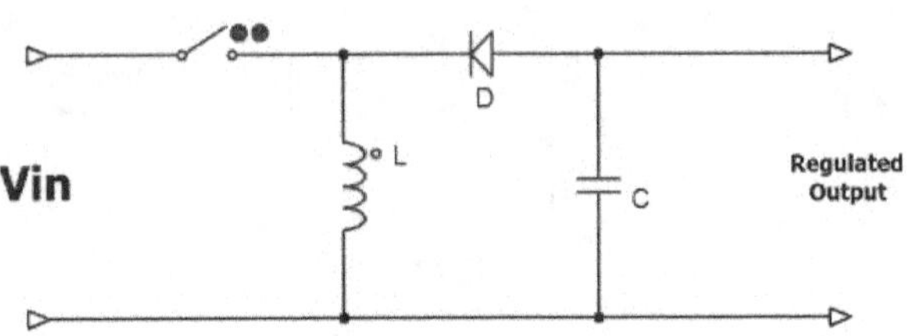

At the point when the switch is ON the diode acts as turned around one-sided and inductor stores vitality and when the switch is OFF inductor begin discharging the vitality with the converse extremity, which charges the capacitor. At the point when the vitality put away in inductor becomes zero the capacitor begins releasing into the heap with invert extremity. Because of this buck-support controller additionally called as modifying controller.

The yield voltage is characterized as

Vout = Vin (D / 1-D)

Where, D is the Duty cycle

Subsequently, if the Duty Cycle is low the controller carries on as the Buck Regulator and when the Duty Cycle is high the controller acts as the Boost Regulator.

Pragmatic Example for Regulator Circuits

Positive Linear Voltage Regulator Circuit

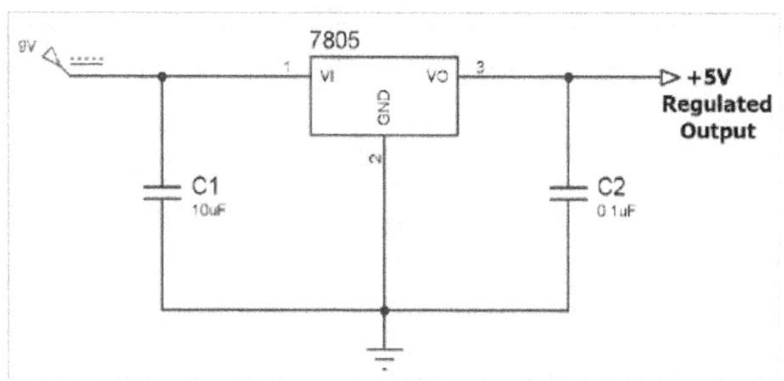

We have structured a positive straight voltage controller circuit utilizing 7805 IC. This IC has all the hardware to give the 5volt managed supply. The information voltage ought to be atleast more than 2v from the evaluated esteem like for LM7805 we ought to atleast give 7v.

Unregulated info voltage is provided to the IC and we get managed voltage at the yield terminal. The name of the IC characterizes its capacity, 78 speak to the positive sign and 05 speaks to the estimation of the directed yield voltage. As you find in the circuit graph we are offering 9V to the 7805IC and getting directed +5V at the yield. The capacitor C1 and C2 are utilized for filtration.

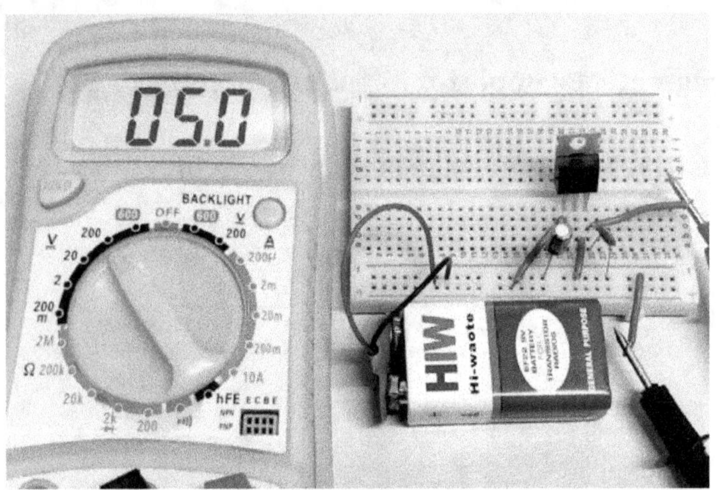

Zener Voltage Regulator Circuit

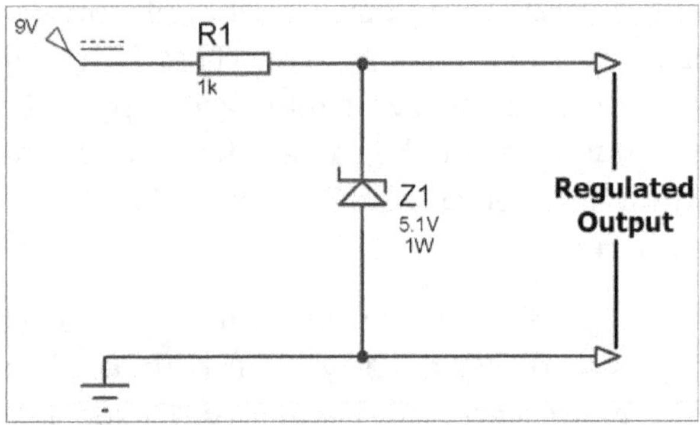

Here, we have structured a Zener Voltage Regulator utilizing 5.1V of Zener diode. The Zener diode functions as the detecting component. At the point when the stock voltage surpasses its breakdown voltage, its beginning leading backward heading and keeps up a similar voltage across it along with stream back the additional current, in this way give the steady yield voltage. In this circuit we are giving 9V of info voltage and getting about 5.1 voltage of directed yield.

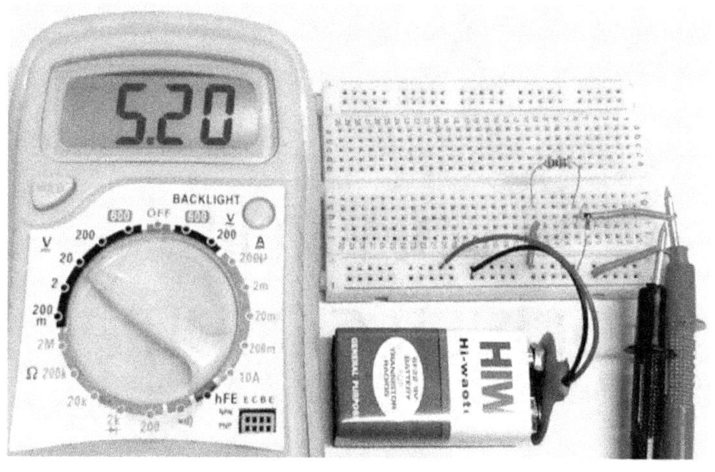

5. SOLENOID DRIVER CIRCUIT

Solenoids are ordinarily utilized actuators in many procedure computerization frameworks. There are numerous kinds of solenoid, for example there are solenoid valves can be used to open otherwise close water or gas pipe lines and there are solenoid uncloggers are used to make direct movement. One normal utilization of solenoid that the majority of us would have gone over is the ding-dong entryway chime. The Door chime has an unclogger type solenoid loop inside it, which when invigorated by AC power source will move a little bar here and there. This bar will hit the metal plates put on either side of the solenoid to create the relieving ding dong sound.

In case there are numerous kinds of solenoid components accessible, the most fundamental thing continues as before. That is, it has a curl twisted over a metal (conductive) material. At the point when the loop is invigorated this conductive material is exposed to some mechanical development which is then turned around through a spring or other component when de-stimulated. Since the solenoid includes loop they regularly expend a lot of ebb and flow making it obligatory to have some sort of driver circuit to work it. In this instructional exercise we will figure out how to construct driver circuit to control a Solenoid valve.

Materials Required

- Solenoid Valve

- 12V Adapter

- 7805 Regulator IC

- IRF540N MOSFET

- Diode IN4007

- 0.1uf Capacious

- 1k and 10k Resistors

- Associating wires

- Breadboard

What is a Solenoid and how can it work?

A solenoid is a gadget that changes over electrical vitality into mechanical vitality. It has a curl twisted over a conductive material, this set-up goes about as an electromagnet. The benefit of an electromagnet over normal magnet is that it very well may be turned on or off when required by empowering the curl. In this manner when the loop is empowered at that point as per faradays law the current conveying conductor has an attractive field around it, since the conductor is a curl the attractive field is sufficiently able to polarize the material and make a straight movement.

During this procedure the curl draws a lot of current

and furthermore creates hysteresis issue, henceforth it is unimaginable to expect to drive a Solenoid loop legitimately however a rationale circuit. Here we are utilizing a 12V solenoid valve which is ordinarily utilized in controlling the progression of fluids. The solenoid draws a nonstop ebb and flow of 700mA when empowered and a pinnacle of almost 1.2A so we need to consider these things while structuring the driver circuit for this specific Solenoid valve.

Schematic Diagram

The total circuit chart for Solenoid driver circuit is appeared in the picture beneath. We will comprehend why it is structured in this way, once subsequent to investigating the total circuit.

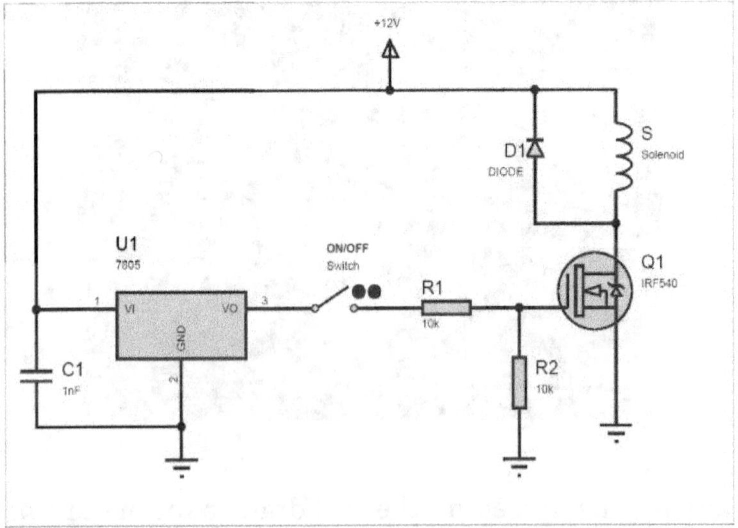

As should be obvious the circuit is extremely straightforward and simple to manufacture, henceforth we can test this using a little breadboard association. A solenoid would simple be able to be turned on by fueling 12V over its terminals and killed by driving it off. To control this turn on and off procedure using an advanced circuit we need an exchanging gadget like the MOSFET and in this manner it is the significant part in this circuit. Coming up next are the parameters that you need to check while choosing the MOSFET.

Entryway Source Threshold Voltage VGS(th): This is the voltage that must be provided to MOSFET to turn it ON. Here the limit voltage esteem is 4V and we are providing a voltage of 5V which is all that could possibly be needed to turn on the MOSFET totally

Nonstop Drain current: The ceaseless channel current is the most extreme current that can be permitted to course through a circuit. Here our solenoid expends a most extreme pinnacle current of 1.2A and the rating of our MOSFET is 10A at 5V Vgs. So we are more than safe with the present rating of the MOSFET. It is constantly prescribed to have some upper peripheral distinction between the genuine worth and evaluated estimation of current.

Channel Source On-State Resistance: When the MOSFET is completely turned on it has some opposition between the Drain and Source pin, this obstruction is called as on state obstruction. The estimation of this ought to be as low as conceivable else there will be colossal voltage drop (ohms law) over the pins bringing about not adequate voltage for the Solenoid to turn on. The estimation of on-state obstruction here is just 0.077?.

You can take a gander at the datasheet of your MOSFET in the event that you are structuring the circuit for some other Solenoid application. A 7805 Linear Regulator IC is utilized to change over the 12V information supply to 5V, this voltage is then given to the Gate pin of the MOSFET when the switch is squeezed however a 1K current restricting resistor. At the point when the switch isn't squeezed the door pin is gotten down to ground through a 10k Resistor. This keeps the MOSFET killed when the switch isn't squeezed. At long last a diode is included enemy of equal heading to forestall the solenoid curl from releasing into the force circuit.

Working of Solenoid Driver Circuit

Since we have seen how the Driver circuit functions lets test the circuit by building it on a bread board. I have utilized a 12V connector for powers supply and my equipment arrangement looks something like this when finished.

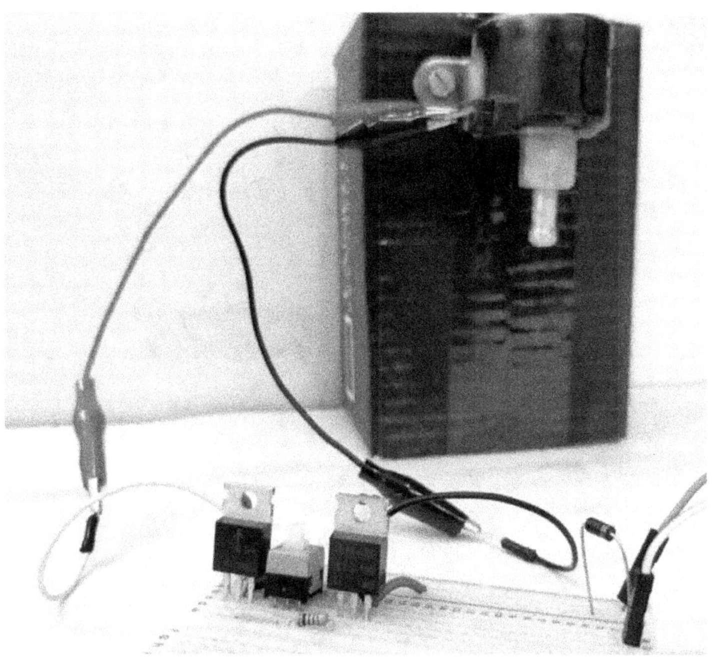

At the point when the switch in the middle of is squeezed the +5V supply is given to the MOSFET and it turns on the Solenoid. At the point when the switch is squeezed again it detaches the +5V supply to MOS-FET and the solenoid returns to off state. The killing on and the solenoid can be seen by the clicking sound made by it, yet to make it more intriguing I have associated the solenoid valve to a water pipe. Of course when solenoid is off the worth is shut and thus no water comes out through opposite end. At that point when the solenoid is turned on the worth gets open and water streams out.

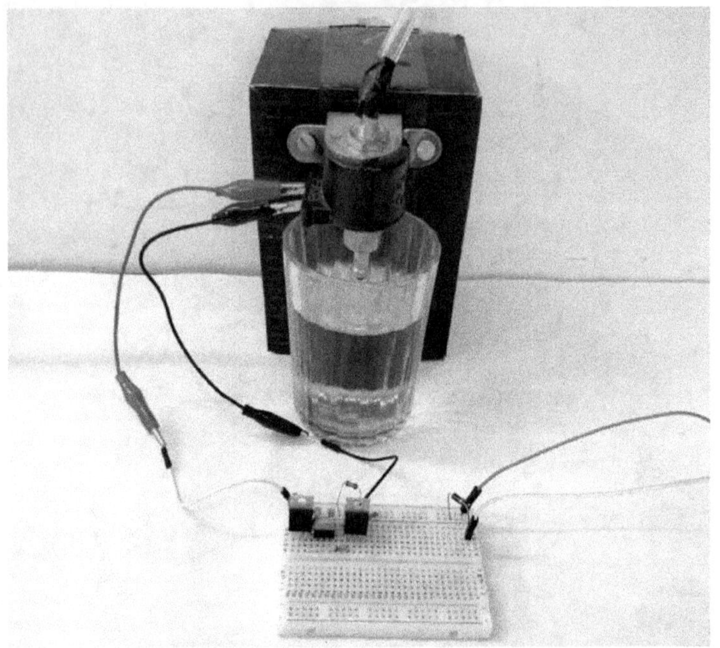

Expectation you comprehended the venture and appreciated structure it.

6. 12V TO 5V BUCK CONVERTER CIRCUIT UTILIZING MC34063

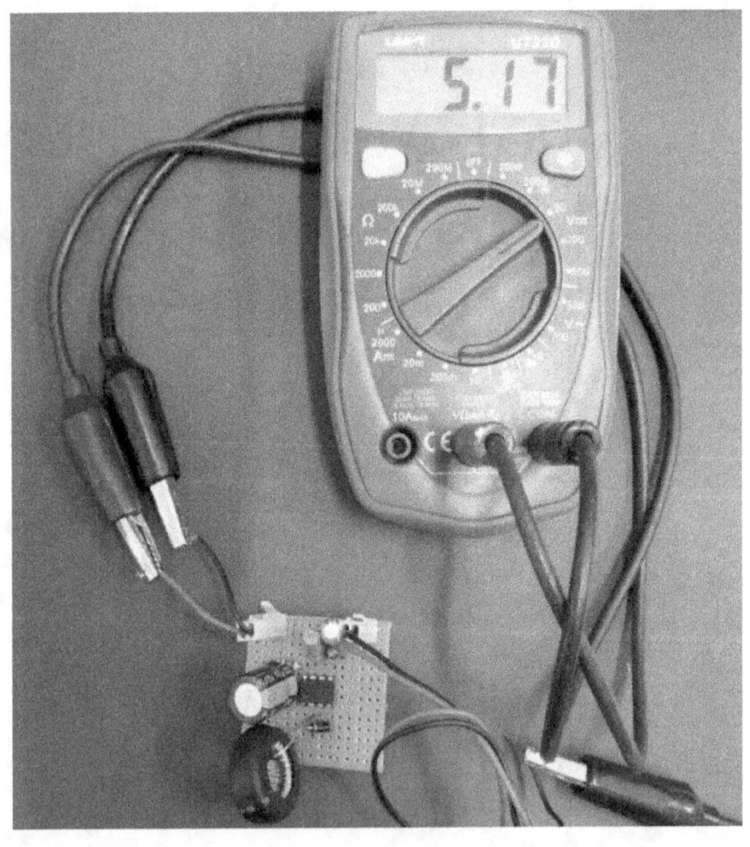

In the past instructional exercise, we exhibited definite plan of Boost Converter utilizing MC34063, where a 3.7V to 5V support converter was structured. Here we perceive how to change over 12V to 5V. As we know that definite 5V batteries are not constantly accessible, and now and again we need higher voltage and lower voltage simultaneously to drive various pieces of circuit, so we utilize higher voltage (12v) source as the principle power source and venture down this voltage to bring down voltage (5v) any place required. This is why, a Buck Converter Circuit is utilized in numerous gadgets applications which drops the information voltage according to the heap prerequisite.

There are bunches of decisions accessible in this section; as found in the past instructional exercise, MC34063 is one of those most famous exchanging controllers accessible in such portion. MC34063 can be arranged in three mode, Buck, Boost, along with Inverting. We will utilize the Buck setup to change over the 12V DC source to 5V DC with 1A yield current capacity. We have presently assembled straightforward Buck Converter circuit utilizing MOSFET; you can likewise check a lot progressively helpful force gadgets circuits here.

IC MC34063

MC34063 pinout outline has been appeared in the beneath picture. On the left side the inside circuit of MC34063 is appeared, and on the opposite side the pinout graph is appeared.

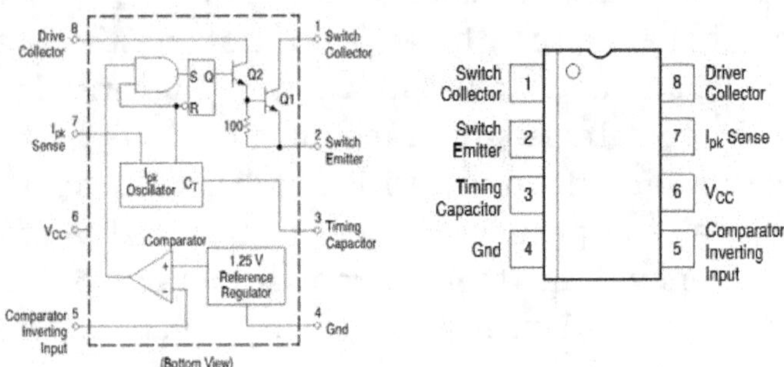

MC34063 is a 1.5A Step up or step down otherwise upsetting controller, because of DC voltage change property, MC34063 is a DC-DC converter IC.

This IC gives following highlights in its 8 pin bundle

- Temperature remunerated reference

- Current breaking point circuit

- Controlled Duty cycle oscillator with a functioning high ebb and flow driver yield switch.

- Acknowledge 3.0V to 40V DC.

- Can be worked at 100 KHz exchanging recurrence with a 2% resistance.

- Low Standby current

- Customizable yield voltage

Additionally, regardless of these highlights, it is broadly accessible and it is abundantly cost proficient than different ICs accessible in such fragment.

In the past instructional exercise, we planned voltage step-up circuit utilizing MC34063 to support 3.7V Lithium battery voltage to 5.5V, in this instructional exercise we will structure 12V to 5V Buck converter.

Computing the Components' Values for Boost Converter

On the off chance that we check the datasheet, we can view the total equation graph is available to compute the ideal qualities required according to our necessity. Here is the recipe sheet accessible inside the datasheet, and the progression up circuit is likewise appeared.

MC34063A, MC33063A, NCV33063A

Calculation	Step–Up	Step–Down	Voltage–Inverting
t_{on}/t_{off}	$\dfrac{V_{out} + V_F - V_{in(min)}}{V_{in(min)} - V_{sat}}$	$\dfrac{V_{out} + V_F}{V_{in(min)} - V_{sat} - V_{out}}$	$\dfrac{|V_{out}| + V_F}{V_{in} - V_{sat}}$
$(t_{on} + t_{off})$	$\dfrac{1}{f}$	$\dfrac{1}{f}$	$\dfrac{1}{f}$
t_{off}	$\dfrac{t_{on} + t_{off}}{\dfrac{t_{on}}{t_{off}} + 1}$	$\dfrac{t_{on} + t_{off}}{\dfrac{t_{on}}{t_{off}} + 1}$	$\dfrac{t_{on} + t_{off}}{\dfrac{t_{on}}{t_{off}} + 1}$
t_{on}	$(t_{on} + t_{off}) - t_{off}$	$(t_{on} + t_{off}) - t_{off}$	$(t_{on} + t_{off}) - t_{off}$
C_T	$4.0 \times 10^{-5}\, t_{on}$	$4.0 \times 10^{-5}\, t_{on}$	$4.0 \times 10^{-5}\, t_{on}$
$I_{pk(switch)}$	$2I_{out(max)}\left(\dfrac{t_{on}}{t_{off}} + 1\right)$	$2I_{out(max)}$	$2I_{out(max)}\left(\dfrac{t_{on}}{t_{off}} + 1\right)$
R_{sc}	$0.3/I_{pk(switch)}$	$0.3/I_{pk(switch)}$	$0.3/I_{pk(switch)}$
$L_{(min)}$	$\left(\dfrac{V_{in(min)} - V_{sat}}{I_{pk(switch)}}\right) t_{on(max)}$	$\left(\dfrac{V_{in(min)} - V_{sat} - V_{out}}{I_{pk(switch)}}\right) t_{on(max)}$	$\left(\dfrac{V_{in(min)} - V_{sat}}{I_{pk(switch)}}\right) t_{on(max)}$
C_O	$9\,\dfrac{I_{out} t_{on}}{V_{ripple(pp)}}$	$\dfrac{I_{pk(switch)}(t_{on} + t_{off})}{8 V_{ripple(pp)}}$	$9\,\dfrac{I_{out} t_{on}}{V_{ripple(pp)}}$

V_{sat} = Saturation voltage of the output switch.
V_F = Forward voltage drop of the output rectifier.

The following power supply characteristics must be chosen:

V_{in} – Nominal input voltage.
V_{out} – Desired output voltage, $|V_{out}| = 1.25\left(1 + \dfrac{R2}{R1}\right)$
I_{out} – Desired output current.
f_{min} – Minimum desired output switching frequency at the selected values of V_{in} and I_O.
$V_{ripple(pp)}$ – Desired peak–to–peak output ripple voltage. In practice, the calculated capacitor value will need to be increased due to its equivalent series resistance and board layout. The ripple voltage should be kept to a low value since it will directly affect the line and load regulation.

NOTE: For further information refer to Application Note AN920A/D and AN954/D.

Design Formula Table

Here is the schematic without those parts esteem, which will be utilized moreover with the MC34063.

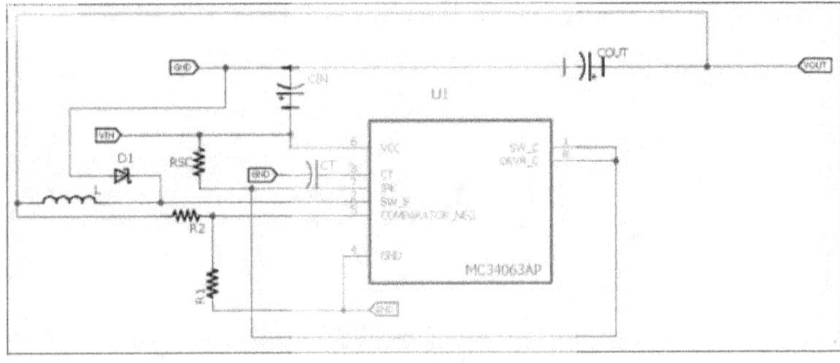

We will figure the qualities which are required for our structure. We can make the estimations from the equations gave in the datasheet or we can utilize the exceed expectations sheet gave by ON Semiconductor's site.

Here is the connection of the exceed expectations sheet.

https://www.onsemi.com/bar/Collateral/ MC34063%20DWS.XLS

Steps to ascertain those parts esteems

Stage 1:- First, we have to choose the Diode. We will pick generally accessible diode 1N5819. In accordance with the datasheet, at 1A forward current the forward voltage of the diode will be 0.60 V.

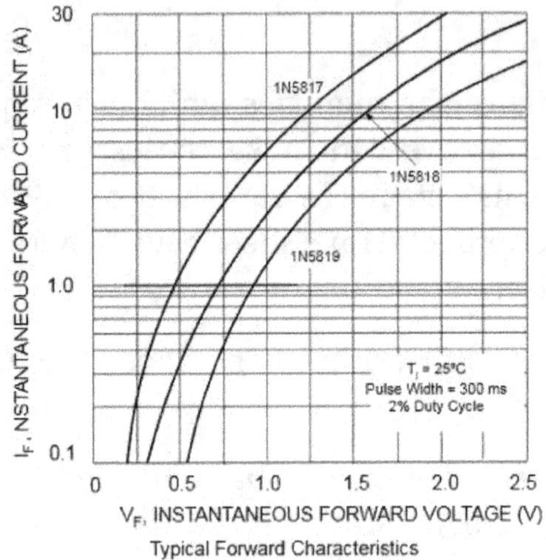

Typical Forward Characteristics

Stage 2:- We initially compute inductor and exchanging present as it will be required for additional count. Our Average Inductor current will be the pinnacle inductor current. In this way, for our situation Inductor current is:

$$IL(avg) = 1A$$

Stage 3:- Now it is the ideal opportunity for the wave current of the inductor. A commonplace inductor utilize 20-40% of the Average yield current. In this way, in the event that we pick the inductor swell current 30%, it will be 1A * 30% = 0.30A

Stage 4:- The Switching top current will be IL(avg) + Iripple/2 = 1 + .30/2 = 1.15A

Stage 5:- We will figure the tON/tOFF utilizing the recipe underneath

$$\frac{Vout+Vf}{Vin(\text{min})-\,Vsat-Vout}$$

For this, our Vout is 5V, and forward voltage of the diode (Vf) is 0.60V. Our base information Voltage Vin (min) is 12V and the immersion voltage is (1V in the datasheet). By, assembling this all we get

(5+0.60) / (12-1-5) = 0.93

So, t_{ON}/t_{OFF} = .93uS

Stage 6:- Now we will ascertain the Ton + Toff time, according to the equation Ton + Toff = 1/f

We will choose a lower exchanging recurrence, 40Khz.

So, **Ton + Toff = 1 / 40Khz = 25us**

Stage 7:- Now we will figure the Toff time. As we determined the Ton + Toff and Ton/Toff already, the figuring will be simpler at this point,

$$\text{Toff} = \frac{Ton + Toff}{\frac{Ton}{Toff} + 1}$$

$$\text{Toff} = \frac{25us}{.93 + 1} = 12.95uS$$

Stage 8:- Now the following stage is to ascertain Ton,

> **Ton = (Ton + Toff) – Toff = 25us – 12.95us = 12.05us**

Stage 9:- We have to pick the planning Capacitor Ct, which will be required to create the ideal recurrence.

> **Ct = 4.0 x10^{-5} x Ton = 4.0 x 10^{-5} x 12.05uS = 482pF**

Stage 10:- Depending on those qualities we will figure the Inductor esteem

$$\text{Lmin} = \frac{Vin(\text{min}) - Vsat - Vout}{Ipk} \times Ton$$

$$\text{Lmin} = \frac{(12 - 1 - 5)}{1.15A} \times 12.05uS = 62.87uH$$

Stage 11:- For the 1A current, The Rsc worth will be 0.3/Ipk. In this way, for our prerequisite it will be Rsc = .3/1.15 = .260 Ohms

Stage 12:- Let's ascertain the yield capacitor esteems, we can pick a wave estimation of 100mV (top to top) from the lift yield.

$$Cout = \frac{Ipk\ (Ton+Toff)}{8 \times Vripple(pk-pk)}$$

$$Cout = \frac{1.15 \times 25}{8 \times 100} = 359.375uF$$

We will pick 470uF, 25V. The more capacitor will be utilized, the more wave it will diminish.

Stage 13:- Last we have to compute the voltage criticism resistors esteem. We will pick R1 esteem 2k, So, the R2 worth will be determined as

Vout = 1.25 (1 + R2/R1)

5 = 1.25 (1 + R2 / 2K)

R2 = 6.2k

Buck Converter Circuit Diagram

So in the wake of computing all the qualities. Here is the refreshed schematic

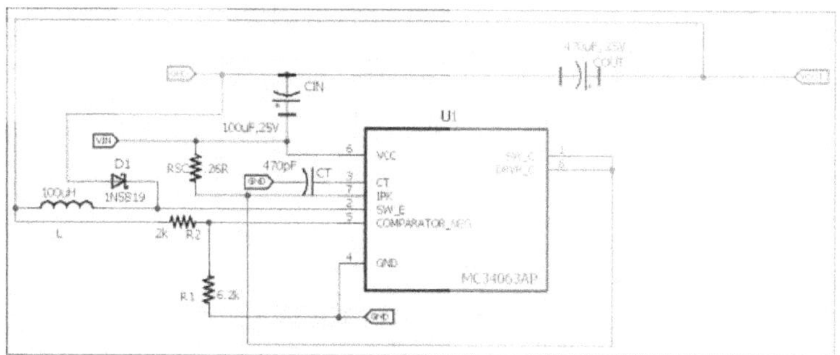

Required parts

- 2 nos relimate connector for information and yield

- 2k resistor-1 nos

- 6.2k resistor-1 nos

- 1N5819-1 nos

- 100uF, 25V and 359.37uF, 25V capacitor (470uF, 25V utilized, close worth chose)- 1 nos each.

- 62.87uH inductor, 1.5A 1 nos. (100uH 2.5A is utilized, it was promptly accessible in advertise)

- 482pF (470pF utilized) earthenware circle capacitor-1 nos

- 12V Power Supply unit with 1.5A Rating.

- MC34063 exchanging controller ic

- .26ohms resistor (.3R, 2W utilized)

- 1 nos veroboard (specked or associated vero can be utilized).

- Welding Iron

- Welding Flux and Soldering wires.

- Extra wires whenever required.

Note: We have utilized 100uh inductor as it is accessible effectively with nearby merchants with the 2.5A current rating. Likewise we have utilized .3R resistor rather .26R.

In the wake of masterminding the segments, weld the segments on Perfboard

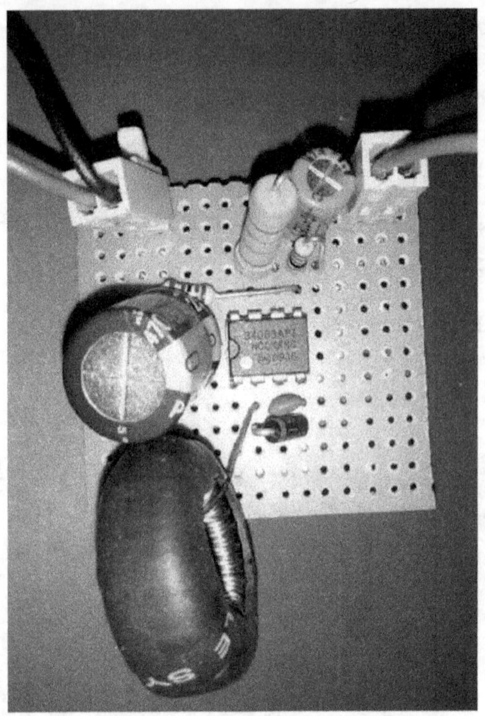

Testing the Buck Converter Circuit

Before testing the circuit we need variable DC burdens to draw the current from the Direct Current power supply. In the little hardware lab where we are trying the circuit, test resistances are a lot higher and because of that, couple of estimation correctnesses are not sufficient.

Oscilloscope is appropriately adjusted however fake clamors, EMI, RF can likewise change the test outcome exactness. Likewise, the Multimeter have +/ -

1% resistances.

Here we will gauge the accompanying things

- Yield wave and voltage at different loads up to 1000mA. Likewise, test the yield voltage at this full burden.

- The effectiveness of the circuit.

- Inert current utilization of the circuit.

- Short out state of the circuit.

- Additionally, what will occur in the event that we over-burden the yield?

Our room temperature is 26 degree Celsius when we tried the circuit.

In the above picture, we can see the DC load. This is a resistive burden and as should be obvious, ten no. of 1 ohm resistors in equal association are the genuine burden, which is associated over a MOS-FET, We will control the MOSFET door and permit the current to course through the resistors. Those resistors convert electrical forces to warm. The outcome comprises of 5 % resilience. Additionally, these load results incorporate the force draw of the load itself, so when no load is being associated across it and controlled utilizing an outside force supply, it will show default 70mA of burden current. For our situation, we determination the heap from outside seat power supply and test the circuit. The last yield will be (Result – 70mA).

The following is our test arrangement; we have associated the load over the circuit, we measure the produce current over the buck controller just as the produce voltage of it. An oscilloscope is likewise associated over the buck converter, so we can likewise check the yield voltage. We are giving 12V contribution from our seat power supply unit.

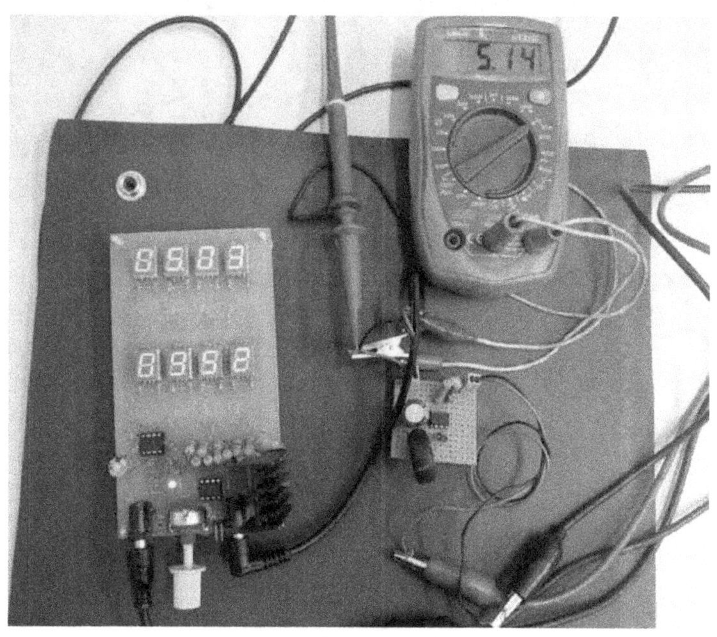

We are drawing .88A or 952mA-70mA = 882mA of current from the yield. The yield voltage is 5.15V.

Now, in the event that we check the top to top wave in the oscilloscope. We can see the yield wave, the wave is 60mV (pk-pk). Which is useful for a 12V to 5V Switching buck converter.

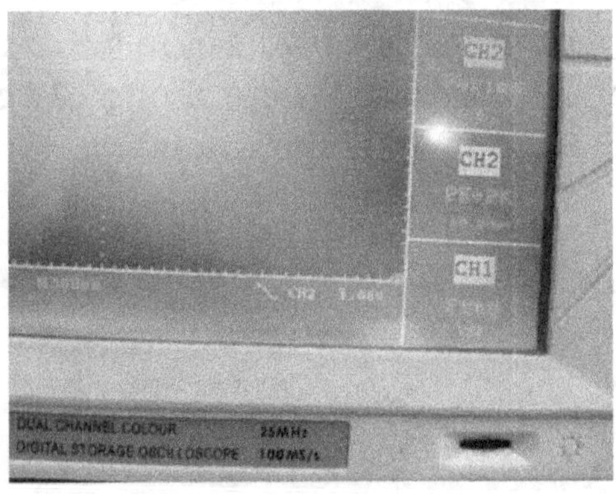

The yield waveform resembles this:

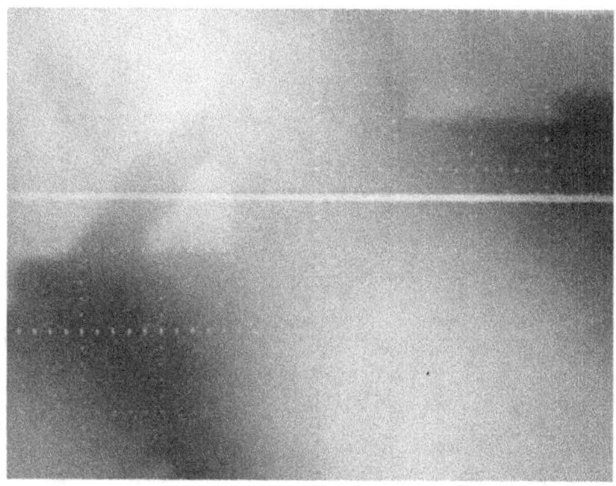

Here is the time span of the yield waveform. It is 500mV per division along with 500uS time allotment.

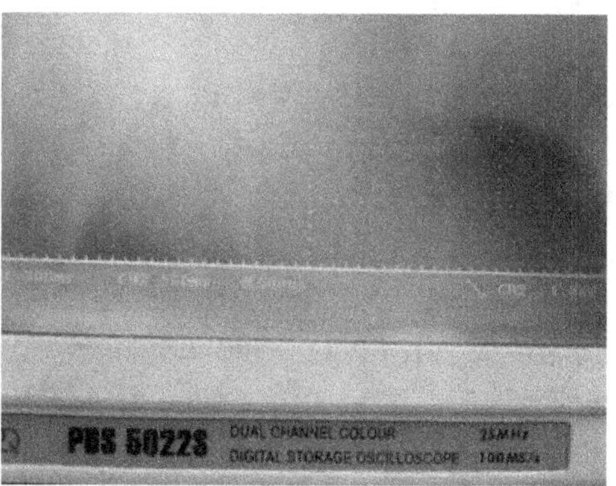

Here is the point by point test report

Time (secs)	Load (mA)	Voltage (V)	Ripple(p-p) (mV)

180	0	5.17	60
180	200	5.16	60
180	400	5.16	60
180	600	5.16	80
180	800	5.15	80
180	982	5.13	80
180	1200	4.33	120

We changed the heap and hung tight for approx 3 minutes, on each progression, to check if the outcomes are steady or not. After 982mA burden the voltage dropped altogether. In different cases from 0 burdens to the 940 mA, the yield voltage dropped was approx .02V, which is very acceptable solidness at full burden. Additionally, after that 982mA burden, the yield voltage is dropped fundamentally. We utilized .3R resistor where .26R was required, because of that, we can draw 982mA of burden current. The MC34063 power supply can't give legitimate solidness at full 1A load as we utilized .3R rather .26R. In any case, 982mA is exceptionally near 1A yield. Additionally, we utilized resistors with 5% resiliences which are most normally accessible at the neighborhood showcase.

We determined the proficiency at 12V fixed info and by changing the heap. Here is the outcome

Input Voltage (V)	Input Current (A)	Input Power (W)	Output Voltage (V)	Output Current (A)	Output Power (W)	Efficiency (n)
12.04	0.12	1.4448	5.17	0.2	1.034	71.56699889
12.04	0.23	2.7692	5.16	0.4	2.064	74.53416149
12.04	0.34	4.0936	5.16	0.6	3.096	75.6302521
12.04	0.45	5.418	5.16	0.8	4.128	76.19047619
12.04	0.53	6.3812	5.15	0.98	5.047	79.09170689

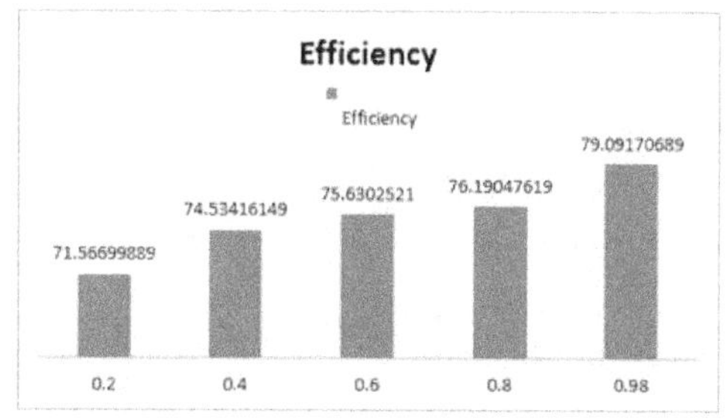

As should be obvious the normal productivity is around 75%, which is a decent yield at this stage.

Inactive current utilization of the circuit is recorded 3.52mA when the heap is 0.

Likewise, we checked for the short out, and we watch Normal in cut off.

After the most extreme yield current edge the yield voltages getting essentially lower and after a specific time, it's drawing near to zero.

Enhancements can be done in this circuit; we can utilize low ESR higher worth capacitor to diminish the yield swell. Additionally, appropriate PCB planning is important.

7. 3.7V TO 5V BOOST CONVERTER CIRCUIT UTILIZING MC34063

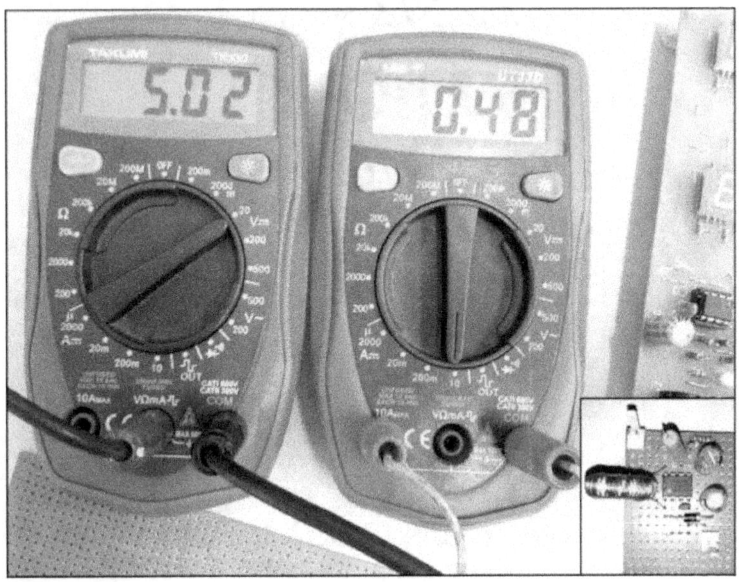

In present day days, Lithium batteries are enhancing the gadgets world. They can be charged exceptionally quick and give great reinforcement, which alongside their low assembling cost settles on lithium batteries the most ideal decision for convenient gadgets. As a solitary cell lithium battery voltage run from least 3.2 voltage to 4.2V, it's hard to control those circuits which requires 5V or more. In such case we need a Boost Converter which will support the voltage in accordance with the heap necessity, more than it's info voltage.

A great deal of decisions accessible in this fragment; MC34063 is most mainstream exchanging controller in such portion. MCP34063 can be arranged in three activity, Buck, Boost and Inverting. We use MC34063 as exchanging Boost controller and will Boost 3.7V lithium battery voltage to 5.5V with 500mA yield current capacities. We have recently constructed Buck Converter circuit to step down the voltage; you can likewise check many intriguing force gadgets extends here.

IC MC34063

MC34063 pinout graph has been appeared in the beneath picture. On the left side the inside circuit of MC34063 is appeared, and on the opposite side the pinout chart is appeared.

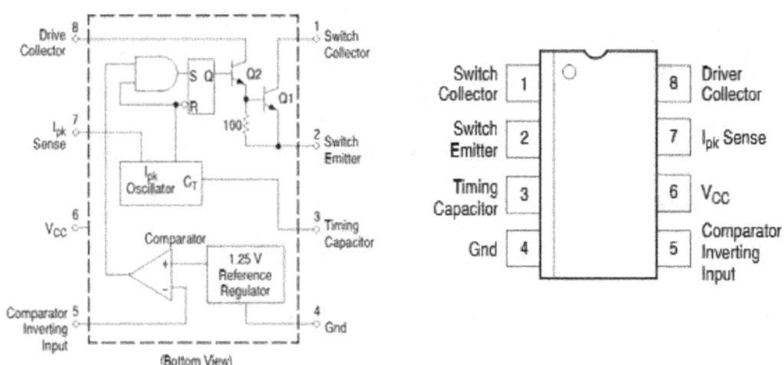

MC34063 is a 1.5A Step up or step down or rearranging controller, because of DC voltage transformation property, MC34063 is a DC-DC converter IC.

This IC gives following highlights in its 8 pin bundle

- Temperature repaid reference

- Current cutoff circuit

- Controlled Duty cycle oscillator with a functioning high ebb and flow driver yield switch.

- Acknowledge 3.0V to 40V DC.

- Can be worked at 100 KHz exchanging recurrence with a 2% resistance.

- Exceptionally low Standby current

- Customizable yield voltage

Additionally, in case highlights, it is generally accessible and it is tremendously cost productive than different ICs accessible in such fragment.

We should structure our progression up circuit utilizing MC34063 to support 3.7V Lithium battery voltage to 5.5V.

Computing the Components' Values for Boost Converter

On the off chance that we check the datasheet, we can

view the total recipe outline is available to ascertain the ideal qualities required according to our necessity. Here is the equation sheet accessible inside the datasheet, and the progression up circuit is additionally appeared.

MC34063A, MC33063A, NCV33063A

Calculation	Step–Up	Step–Down	Voltage–Inverting
t_{on}/t_{off}	$\dfrac{V_{out} + V_F - V_{in(min)}}{V_{in(min)} - V_{sat}}$	$\dfrac{V_{out} + V_F}{V_{in(min)} - V_{sat} - V_{out}}$	$\dfrac{|V_{out}| + V_F}{V_{in} - V_{sat}}$
$(t_{on} + t_{off})$	$\dfrac{1}{f}$	$\dfrac{1}{f}$	$\dfrac{1}{f}$
t_{off}	$\dfrac{t_{on} + t_{off}}{\frac{t_{on}}{t_{off}} + 1}$	$\dfrac{t_{on} + t_{off}}{\frac{t_{on}}{t_{off}} + 1}$	$\dfrac{t_{on} + t_{off}}{\frac{t_{on}}{t_{off}} + 1}$
t_{on}	$(t_{on} + t_{off}) - t_{off}$	$(t_{on} + t_{off}) - t_{off}$	$(t_{on} + t_{off}) - t_{off}$
C_T	$4.0 \times 10^{-5}\, t_{on}$	$4.0 \times 10^{-5}\, t_{on}$	$4.0 \times 10^{-5}\, t_{on}$
$I_{pk(switch)}$	$2 I_{out(max)} \left(\dfrac{t_{on}}{t_{off}} + 1 \right)$	$2 I_{out(max)}$	$2 I_{out(max)} \left(\dfrac{t_{on}}{t_{off}} + 1 \right)$
R_{sc}	$0.3/I_{pk(switch)}$	$0.3/I_{pk(switch)}$	$0.3/I_{pk(switch)}$
$L_{(min)}$	$\left(\dfrac{(V_{in(min)} - V_{sat})}{I_{pk(switch)}} \right) t_{on(max)}$	$\left(\dfrac{(V_{in(min)} - V_{sat} - V_{out})}{I_{pk(switch)}} \right) t_{on(max)}$	$\left(\dfrac{(V_{in(min)} - V_{sat})}{I_{pk(switch)}} \right) t_{on(max)}$
C_O	$9 \dfrac{I_{out} t_{on}}{V_{ripple(pp)}}$	$\dfrac{I_{pk(switch)}(t_{on} + t_{off})}{8 V_{ripple(pp)}}$	$9 \dfrac{I_{out} t_{on}}{V_{ripple(pp)}}$

V_{sat} = Saturation voltage of the output switch.
V_F = Forward voltage drop of the output rectifier.

The following power supply characteristics must be chosen:

V_{in} – Nominal input voltage.
V_{out} – Desired output voltage, $|V_{out}| = 1.25 \left(1 + \dfrac{R2}{R1} \right)$
I_{out} – Desired output current.
f_{min} – Minimum desired output switching frequency at the selected values of V_{in} and I_O.
$V_{ripple(pp)}$ – Desired peak–to–peak output ripple voltage. In practice, the calculated capacitor value will need to be increased due to its equivalent series resistance and board layout. The ripple voltage should be kept to a low value since it will directly affect the line and load regulation.

NOTE: For further information refer to Application Note AN920A/D and AN954/D.

Design Formula Table

Here is the schematic without those parts esteem, which will be utilized moreover with the MC34063.

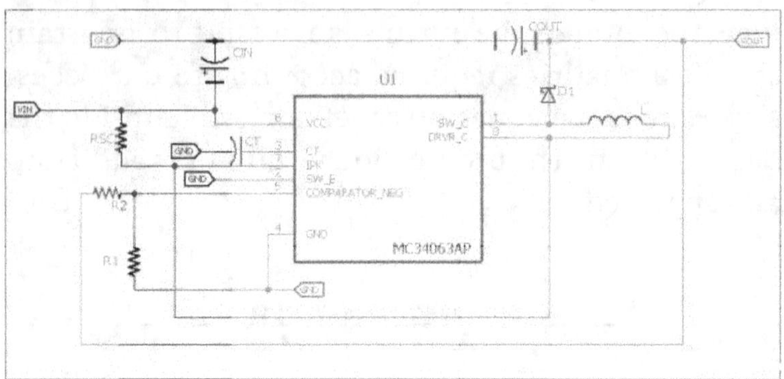

Presently we will figure the qualities which are required for our structure. We can do the counts from the equations gave in the datasheet or we can utilize the exceed expectations sheet gave by ON Semiconductor's site. Here is the connection of the exceed expectations sheet.

https://www.onsemi.com/bar/Collateral/ MC34063%20DWS.XLS

Steps to ascertain those segments esteems

Stage 1:- First we have to choose the Diode. We will pick generally accessible diode 1N5819. In accordance with the datasheet, at 1A forward current the forward voltage of the diode will be 0.60 V.

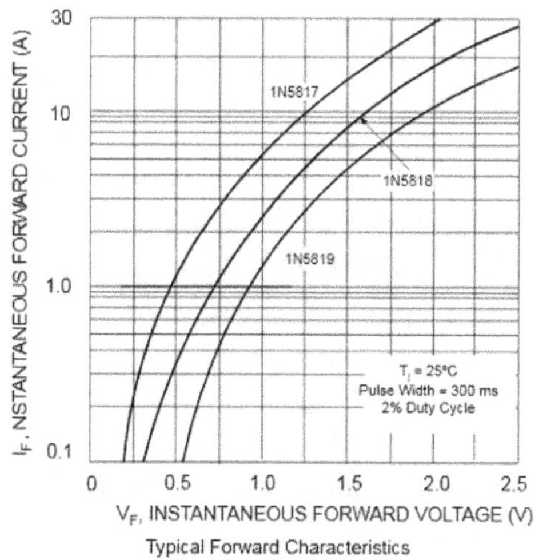

Typical Forward Characteristics

Stage 2:- We will figure the utilizing the equation

$$\frac{Vout + Vf - Vin\,(min)}{Vin(min) - Vsat}$$

For this, our Vout is 5.5V, Forward voltage of the diode (Vf) is 0.60V. Our base Voltage Vin (min) is 3.2V as this is the least adequate voltage from a solitary cell battery. What's more, for the immersion voltage of the yield switch (Vsat), it is (1V in the datasheet). By, assembling this all we get

(5.5+0.60-3.2 / 3.2-1) = 0.9

So, t_{ON} / t_{OFF} = 1.31

Stage 3:- No we will figure the Ton + Toff time, according to the equation Ton + Toff = 1/f

We will choose lower exchanging recurrence, 50Khz.

So, Ton + Toff = 1 / 50Khz = 20us

So our Ton + Toff is 20uS

Stage 4:- Now we will figure the Toff time.

$$T_{off} = (T_{on} + T_{off} / (T_{on}/T_{off})+1)$$

As we determined the Ton + Toff and Ton/Toff already, the estimation will be simpler at this point,

Toff = 20us / 1.31+1 = 8.65us

Stage 5:- Now the subsequent stage is to figure Ton,

$$T_{on} = (T_{on} + T_{off}) - T_{off} = 20us - 8.65us = 11.35us$$

Stage 6:- We should pick the planning Capacitor Ct, which will be reqired to create the ideal recurrence. Ct = 4.0 x 10-5 x Ton = 4.0 x 10-5 x 11.35uS = 454pF

Stage 7:- Now we have to ascertain the Average Inductor current or

$$\text{IL(avg)}. \text{ IL(avg)} = \text{Iout(max)} \times ((T_{on}/T_{off}) + 1)$$

Our greatest yield current will be 500mA. Along these lines, the normal Inductor current will be .5A x (1.31 + 1) = 1.15A.

Stage 8:- Now it is the ideal opportunity for the wave current of the inductor. A run of the mill inductor utilize 20-40% of the Average yield current. In this way, on the off chance that we pick the inductor swell current 30%, it will be 1.15 * 30% = 0.34A

Stage 9:- The Switching top current will be IL(avg) + Iripple/2 = 1.15 + .34/2 = 1.32A

Stage 10:- Depending on those qualities we will figure the Inductor esteem

$$\text{Lmin} = \frac{Vin(min) - Vsat}{Ipk} \times Ton$$

$$\text{Lmin} = \frac{(3.2 - 1)}{1.32A} \times 11.35uS = 18.91uH$$

Stage 11:- For the 500mA current, The Rsc worth will be 0.3/Ipk. Thus, for our necessity it will be Rsc = .3/1.32 = .22 Ohms

Stage 12:- Let's compute the yield capacitor esteems

$$\text{Cout} = 9 \times \frac{Iout \times Ton}{Vripple(pk-pk)}$$

We can pick a wave estimation of 250mV (top to top) from the lift yield.

So, Cout = 9*(0.5*11.35us / 0.25) = 204.3uF

We will pick 220uF, 12V. The more capacitor will be utilized the more wave it will diminish.

Stage 13:- Last we have to ascertain the voltage criticism resistors esteem. Vout = 1.25 (1 + R2/R1)

We will pick R1 esteem 2k, So, the R2 worth will be 5.5 = 1.25 (1 + R2/2k) = 6.8k

We determined all qualities. So beneath is the last schematic:

Lift Converter Circuit Diagram

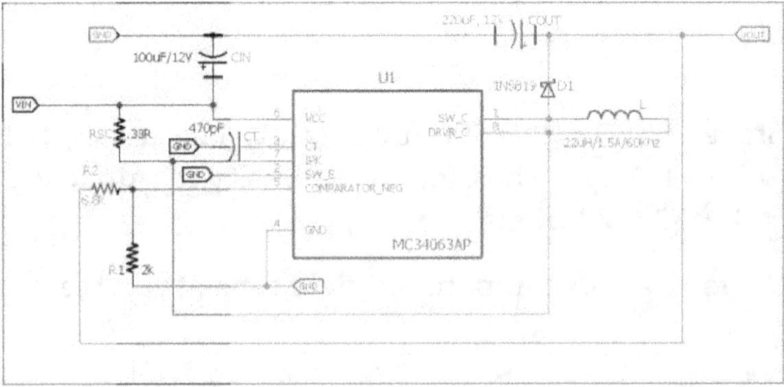

Required Components

- Relimate connector for information and yield 2 nos

- 2k resistor-1 nos

- 6.8k resistor-1 nos

- 1N5819-1nos

- 100uF, 12V and 194.94uF, 12V capacitor (220uF,12V is utilized, close worth chose) 1 nos each.

- 18.91uH inductor, 1.5A - 1 nos. (33uH 2.5A is utilized, it was promptly accessible at our place)

- 454pF (470pF utilized) fired circle capacitor 1 nos

- 1 Lithium particle or Lithium polymer battery Single cell or equal cell relying upon the battery limit with regards to reinforcement related issue in required tasks.

- MC34063 exchanging controller IC

- .24ohms resistor (.3R, 2W utilized)

- 1 nos? Veroboard (specked or associated vero can be utilized).

- Fastening Iron

- Fastening Flux and Soldering wires.

- Extra wires whenever required.

Note: We have utilized 33uh inductor as it is accessible effectively with neighborhood sellers with the 2.5A current rating. Additionally we have utilized .3R resistor rather .22R.

In the wake of organizing the parts, weld the segments on Perfboard

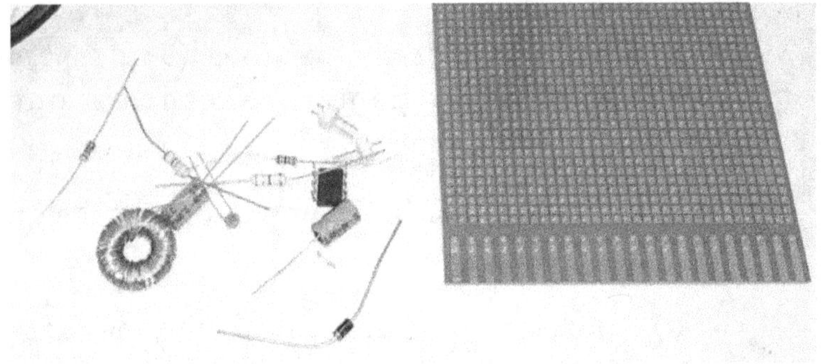

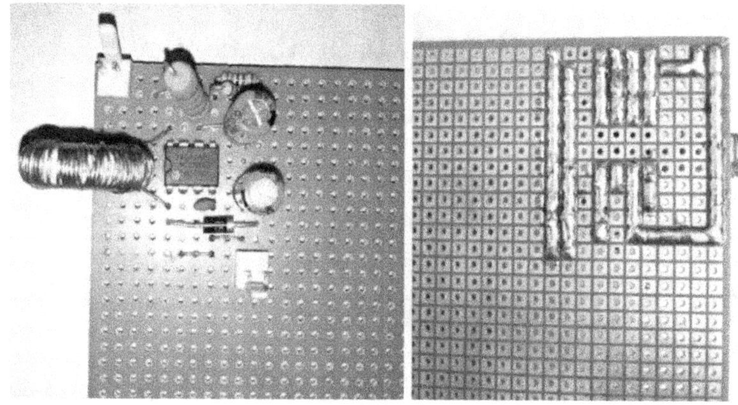

Welding is finished.

Testing the Boost Converter Circuit

Before testing the circuit we need variable Direct Current burdens to draw the current from the Direct Current power supply. In the little hardware lab where we are trying the circuit, test resistances are a lot higher and because of that, couple of estimation correctnesses are not sufficient.

Oscilloscope is appropriately aligned however counterfeit clamors, EMI, RF can likewise change the test outcome exactness. Additionally, the Multimeter have +/- 1% resiliences.

Here we will gauge the accompanying things

- Yield wave and voltage at different loads up to 500mA.

- Effectiveness of the circuit.

- Inert current utilization of the circuit.

- Short out state of the circuit.

- Additionally, what will occur in the event that we over-burden the yield?

Our room temperature is 25 degree Celsius where we tried the circuit.

In the above image we can view the DC load. This is a resistive burden and as should be obvious, 10pcs 1 ohm resistors in equal association are the genuine burden associated over a MOSFET, We will control the MOSFET door and permit the current to course through the resistors. Those resistors convert electrical forces to warm. The outcome comprise 5% resilience. Additionally these heap results incorporate the force draw of the heap itself, so when no heap is being drawn by it, it will show default 70mA of burden current. We self discipline the heap from other force supply and test the circuit. The last yield will be (Result – 70mA). We will utilize multimeters with current detecting mode and measure the current. As the meter is in arrangement with the dc load, the heap show won't give the specific outcome due to the shunt resistors voltage drop inside the multimeters. We will record the meter's outcome.

The following is our test arrangement; we have associated the heap over the circuit, we are estimating the yield current over the lift controller just as the yield voltage of it. An oscilloscope is likewise associated over the lift converter, so we can likewise check the yield voltage. A 18650 lithium battery (1S2P – 3.7V 4400mAH) is giving the info voltage.

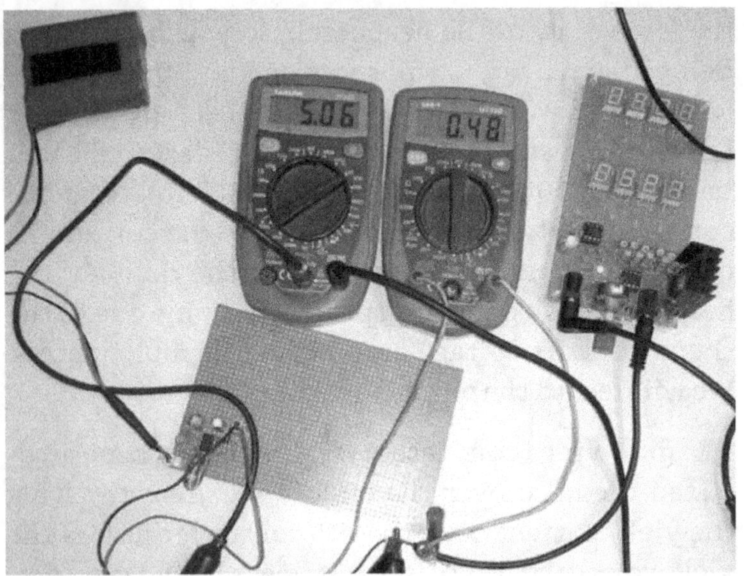

We are drawing .48A or 480-70 = 410mA of current from the yield. The yield voltage is 5.06V.

Now, in case we check the top to top wave in oscilloscope. We can view the yield wave, the wave is 260mV (pk-pk).

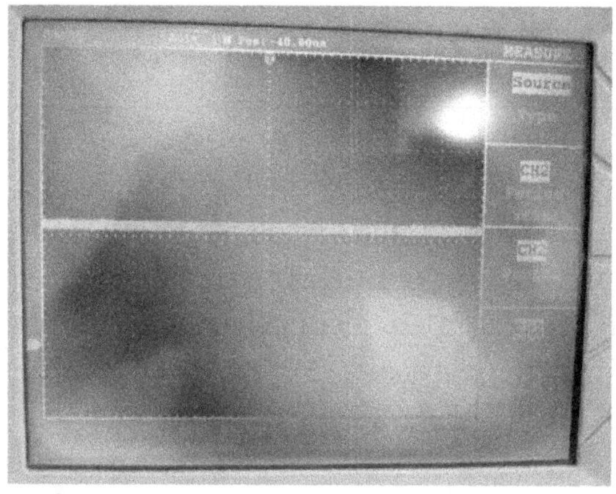

Here is the itemized test report

Time (secs)	Load (mA)	Voltage (V)	Ripple(p-p) (mV)
180	0	5.54	180
180	100	5.46	196
180	200	5.32	208
180	300	5.36	220
180	400	5.16	243
180	500	5.08	258

180	600	4.29	325

We changed the heap and sat tight for approx 3 moment on every progression to check whether the outcomes are steady or not. After 530mA (.53A) load, the voltage dropped altogether. In different cases from 0 burdens to the 500mA the yield voltage dropped .46V.

Testing the circuit with Bench Power Supply

As we can't control the battery voltage, we likewise utilized a variable seat power supply unit to check the yield voltage at least and greatest information voltage(3.3-4.7V) to check whether it is working or not,

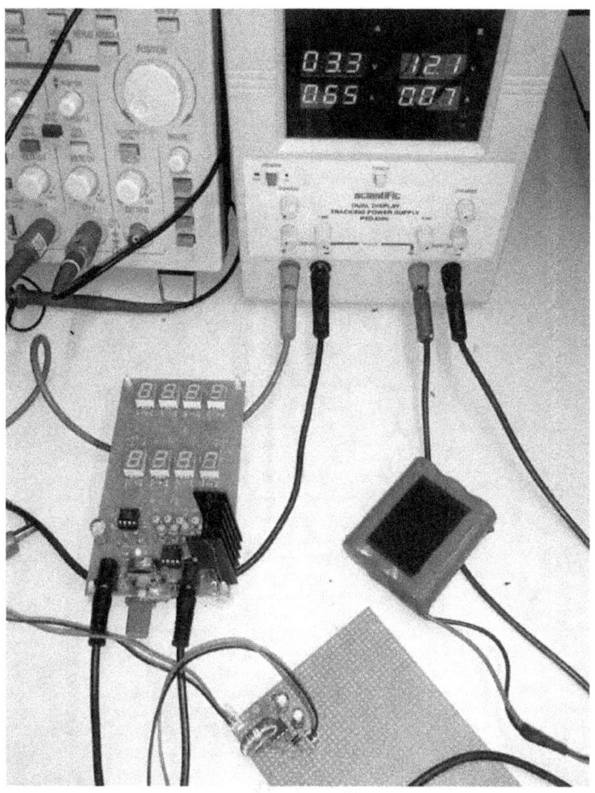

In the above picture seat power supply give 3.3V info voltage. The heap show is demonstrating 5.35V yield at 350mA current draw from the exchanging power supply. As the heap is controlled by the seat power supply, the heap show isn't precise. The present draw result (347mA) additionally comprise the present draw from the seat power supply by the heap itself. The heap is fueled utilizing the seat power supply (12V/60mA). So the genuine current being drawn from the MC34063 yield is 347-60 = 287mA.

We determined the effectiveness at 3.3V by changing the heap, here is the outcome

Input Voltage (V)	Input Current (A)	Input Power (W)	Output Voltage (V)	Output Current (A)	Output Power (W)	Efficiency (n)
3.3	0.46	1.518	5.49	0.183	1.00467	66.1837945
3.3	0.65	2.145	5.35	0.287	1.53545	71.5827506
3.3	0.8	2.64	5.21	0.349	1.81829	68.8746212
3.3	1	3.3	5.12	0.451	2.30912	69.9733333
3.3	1.13	3.729	5.03	0.52	2.6156	70.1421293

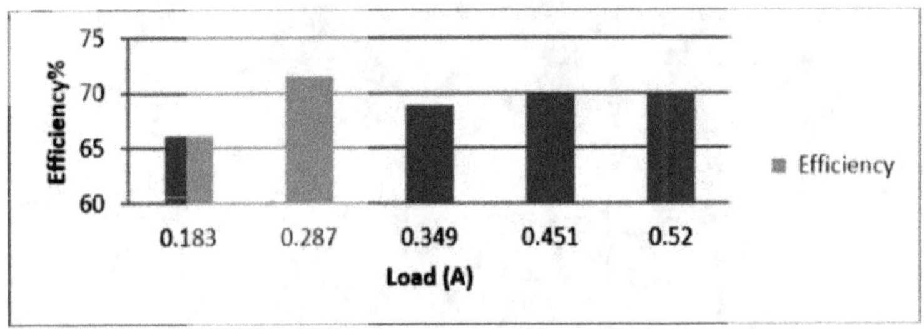

Presently we have changed the voltage to 4.2V info. We are getting 5.41V as yield when we draw 357 – 60 = 297mA of burden.

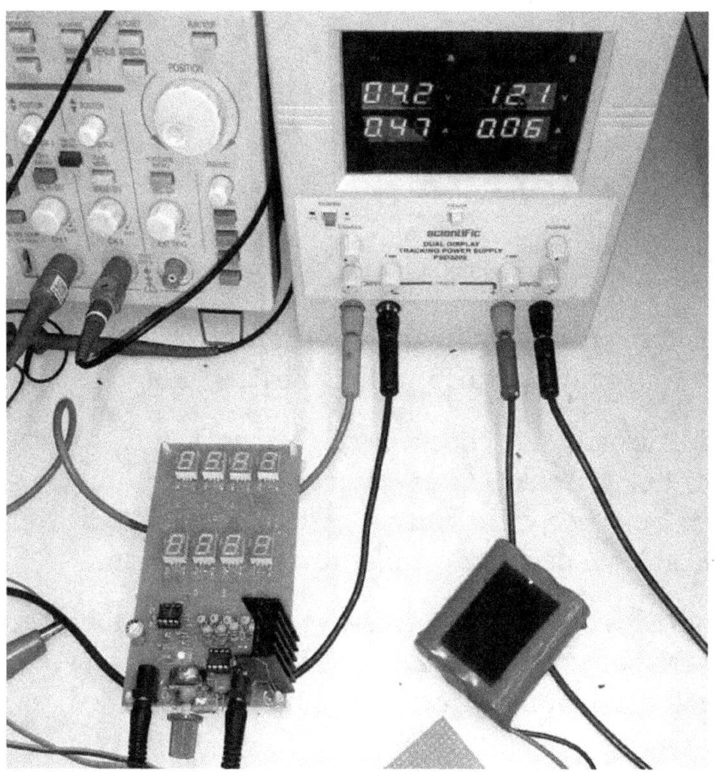

We additionally tried the proficiency. It is marginally superior to the past outcome.

Input Voltage (V)	Input Current (A)	Input Power (W)	Output Voltage (V)	Output Current (A)	Output Power (W)	Efficiency
4.2	0.23	0.966	5.59	0.12	0.6708	69.4409938
4.2	0.37	1.554	5.46	0.21	1.1466	73.7837838
4.2	0.47	1.974	5.41	0.28	1.5148	76.7375887
4.2	0.64	2.688	5.39	0.38	2.0482	76.1979167
4.2	0.8	3.36	5.23	0.47	2.4581	73.1577381

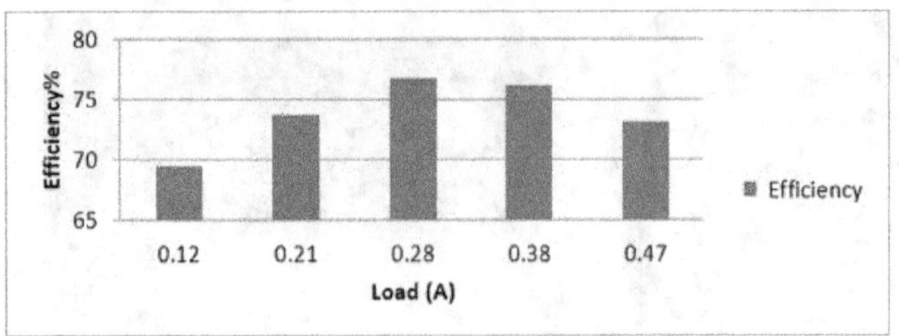

Inactive current utilization of the circuit is recorded 3.47mA at all condition when the heap is 0.

Additionally, we checked for the short out, Normal activity watched. After the most extreme yield current limit the yield voltage getting essentially lower and after a specific time it's drawing near to zero.

Upgrades can be do in this circuit; a low ESR higher worth capacitor can be utilized to decrease the yield swell. Additionally legitimate PCB structuring is essential

8. CROWBAR CIRCUIT

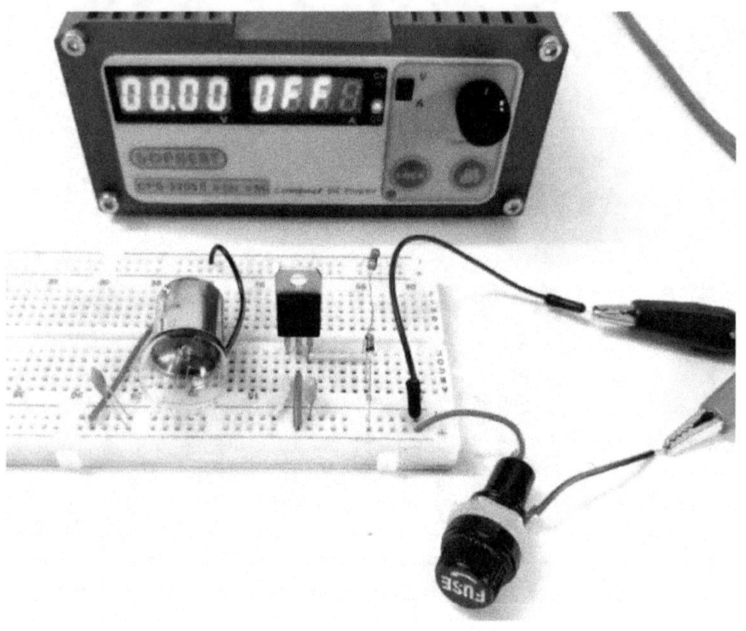

The unwavering quality of any electronic gadget relies upon how well the equipment insurance circuits have been structured. The end client (shopper) is inclined to commit errors and it is the obligation of a decent equipment planner to shield his equipment from any mishappening. There are sufficient sorts of security circuits each with its own particular applications. The most well-known sort of assurance circuits are Over Voltage insurance circuit, Reverse Polarity Protection Circuit, Current flood Protection and Noise security circuits. In this instructional exercise we will examine about the Crowbar Circuit which is a kind of overvoltage security circuit and is regularly utilized in electronic gadgets. We will likewise for all intents along with purposes make this circuit and confirm how it is functioning, all things considered.

Materials Required

- Circuit

- Zener Diode

- Thyristor

- Capacitors

- Resistors

- Schottky Diode

Crowbar Circuit Diagram

The circuit outline of a crowbar circuit is straightforward and simple to construct and execute making it a financially savvy and fast arrangement. The total crowbar circuit chart is demonstrated as follows.

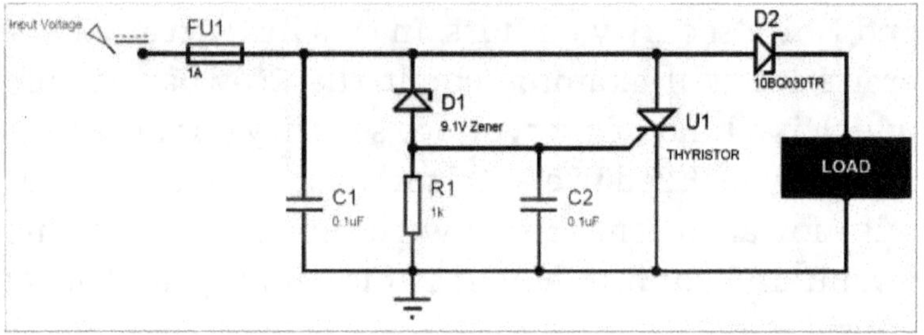

Here the info voltage (blue test) is the voltage which must be checked and the circuit is intended to remove the stockpile when the inventory voltage surpasses 9.1V. We will talk about the capacity of each part in the working area underneath.

Working of Crowbar Circuit

A Crowbar circuit screens the info voltage and when it surpasses the cutoff it makes a short out over the electrical cables and explodes the breaker. When the circuit is blown the force supply will be divided from the heap and therefore keeping it from high voltage. The circuit works by making an immediate short out over the electrical cables, as though a crowbar is dropped among electrical cables of the circuit. Thus it gets its famous name crowbar circuit.

The voltage over which the circuit ought to make a short relies upon the Zener voltage. The circuit comprises of a SCR which is legitimately associated over the Input voltage and ground of the circuit, however this SCR is as a matter of course kept in killed state by establishing the entryway pin of the SCR. At the point when the Input voltage surpasses the Zener voltage the Zener diode starts to lead and henceforth a voltage is provided to the Gate pin of the SCR making it to close the association among the Input Voltage along with Ground in this manner making a short out. This short out will draw a most extreme current from the force supply and explode the wire separating the force supply structure the heap. The total working can likewise be effortlessly comprehended by taking a gander at the GIF picture above.

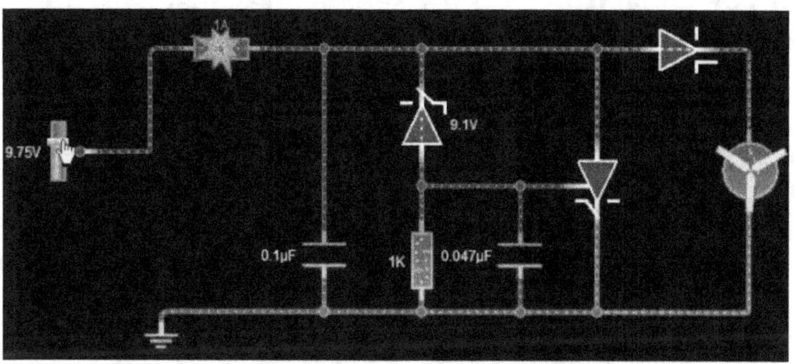

The above picture speaks to how the crowbar circuit reacts precisely when the over-voltage condition happens. As should be obvious the Zener Diode here is appraised for 9.1V yet the information voltage has surpasses the worth and is right now at 9.75V. So the Zener Diode opens and starts to lead by giving a voltage to the Gate pin of the SCR. The SCR at that point starts to direct by shorting the Input voltage and Ground and in this manner explodes the breaker because of most extreme current draw as appeared in GIF above. The capacity of every part in this circuit is clarified beneath.

Breaker: The wire is the fundamental segment in this circuit. The rating of the wire ought to consistently be not exactly the greatest current rating of the SCR and more than the current devoured by the heap. We should likewise ensure that the Power supply can source enough current to break the breaker in occasion if disappointments.

0.1uF Capacitor: This is a separating capacitor; it expels the spikes and other clamor like sounds from the inventory voltage to forestall the circuit structure bogus activating.

9.1V Zener Diode: This diode chooses the over voltage esteem, since here we have utilized a 9.1V Zener diode the circuit will react to any voltage that is over its limit estimation of 9.1V. The Designer can pick the estimation of this resistor as indicated by his needs.

1K Resistor: This is only a draw down resistor which holds the Gate pin of the SCR to ground and consequently keeping it killed until the Zener starts to direct.

47nF Capacitor: Every Power switch like SCR requires a snubber circuit to stifle the voltage spikes during exchanging and keep the SCR from bogus activating. Here we have recently utilized a capacitor to carry out the responsibility. The estimation of the capacitor ought to be sufficiently only to channel the clamor, since high estimation of capacitance will expand the postponement at which the SCR starts to lead in the wake of applying the Gate beat.

Thyristor (SCR): The Thyristor is answerable for making a short out over the force rails. Care ought to be taken with the goal that the SCR can deal with such high estimation of current through it to blow the circuit and harm itself. The Gate voltage of the SCR ought to be not exactly the Zener breakdown voltage. Get familiar with Thyristor here.

Schottky Diode: This diode isn't required and is utilized uniquely for assurance reason. It ensures that we don't get any converse current from the heap side that might harm the assurance circuit. A Schottky diode is utilized rather than a normal diode since it has less voltage drop across it.

Equipment

Since we have comprehended the hypothesis behind the Crowbar circuit, the time has come to get into the pleasant part. That is really constructing the circuit in top of a bread load up and check how it is functioning progressively. The circuit that I am building is for a 12V bulb. This bulb devours about 650mA under typical working voltage of 12V. We will structure the crowbar circuit to check if the voltage surpasses the

12V and in the event that it does we will short the SCR and in this way victory the wire. So here I have utilized a 12V Zener diode and TYN612 Thyristor. The circuit is mounted inside a wire holder, here we have utilized Cartridge Fuse of 500mA rating. The total arrangement is appeared in the image underneath

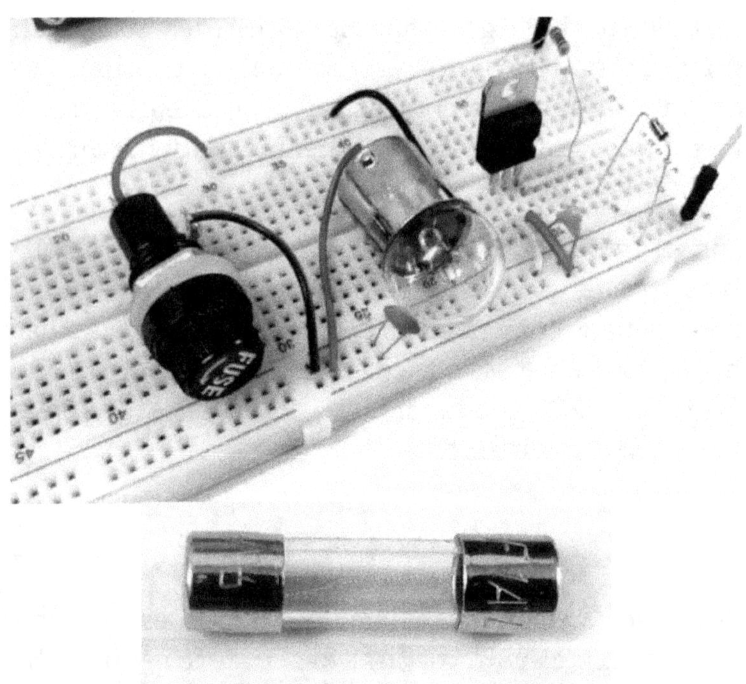

I have utilized a RPS to control the Input voltage, at first the arrangement is tried with 12V and it works fine by turning the bulb on. Later the voltage is raised utilizing the RPS handle accordingly making a short out through the SCR and brushing the circuit which

likewise kills the bulb and seclude it structure the force supply.

Confinements of Crowbar Circuit

Despite the fact that the circuit is broadly utilized it comes with its own restrictions which are recorded beneath

- The overvoltage estimation of the circuit relies simply on the Zener voltage esteem, and just hardly any estimations of Zener diode are accessible.

- The circuit is additionally exposed to commotion issues; this clamor can regularly make a bogus trigger and explode the wire.

- In occasion of overvoltage the circuit blows the breaker and later requires manual assistance to run the heap again when the voltage gets typical.

- The breaker is a mechanical wire which must be supplanted and subsequently expends exertion, time and cash.

9. DC ELECTRONIC FUSE CIRCUIT

Circuit is an imperative assurance gadget for some electronic gadgets. They just screen the current devoured by the circuit/load and in case of perilous current coursing through the circuit the breaker will blow itself and subsequently forestall the heap/circuit structure getting harmed by that high current. This sort of breaker is known as a mechanical wire and there are numerous kinds of wire, for example, quick blow, slow blow and so on, yet they experience the ill effects of one normal downside. At the point when a circuit is passed up the shopper/administrator to do the gadget work typical once more. This is the motivation behind why numerous old electronic gadgets like toaster or electric pot had an extra breaker gave along the item.

To conquer this disadvantage, the mostly of the cutting edge electronic gadgets utilize an Electronic Fuse. An Electronic Fuse fills a similar need of that of a mechanical breaker yet it requires no substitution. It has a force electronic switch inside with closes and opens the circuit as required. In the improbable case of a disappointment the switch is open the circuit and segregate it from the force supply, when the good condition restores the breaker can be reset by simply tapping on a catch. There is no issue of buying an appropriate estimation of breaker and substituting it for the bygone one. Fascinating right?!! In this way, In this instructional exercise we will find out how to develop an Electronic Fuse circuit, how it works and how you could utilize one in your structures.

Electronic Fuse Circuit Diagram:

The total circuit chart for an electronic wire circuit is demonstrated as follows. As appeared in the circuit, it includes just barely any circuits and thus it is anything but difficult to build and execute into our structures.

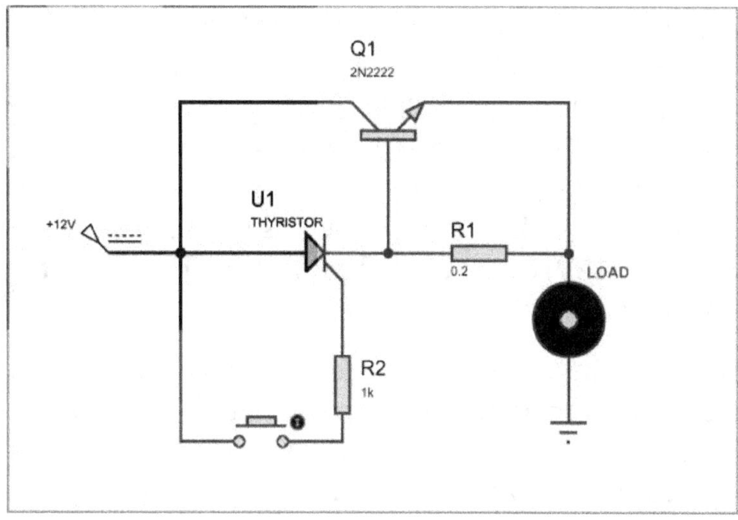

Here the circuit is built to screen the working current of an engine (LOAD), which works on 12V. You can supplant the heap with any circuit whose present you are attempting to screen. The resistor R1 decides how much current can be permitted through the circuit before the circuit responds for an over-current situation. We will investigate the usefulness of every part and how to pick the qualities dependent on your necessity.

Working:

The working of the electronic wire circuit can be effectively comprehended by examine how the SCR functions. Under typical condition the client needs to press the catch to associate the heap to the force supply. At the point when the catch is squeezed the Gate pin of the SCR is associated with source voltage through a 1K Resistor. This will trigger the SCR along with accordingly makes it to close the association between the Cathode and the Anode pin. When the association is shut, current begins to spill out of the Source (+12V) to the heap through the Anode to Cathode pin of the SCR.

At the point when the catch is discharged, the SCR will stay turned on the grounds that there is no recompense circuit to turn it off. In this way the SCR gets locked in ON state and remains there until the present streaming however it goes underneath the holding current of the SCR.

What is implied by Commutation in Thyristors (SCR)?

A Thyristor once turned ON by a sign won't turn OFF without anyone else when the sign is expelled. So to kill a Thyristor we need some outer circuit and this circuit is called as recompense circuit. The way toward turning ON a Thyristor by giving a Gate beat is called as activating and the way toward killing a Thyristor is called as Commutation.

What is holding current in a Thyristor (SCR)?

The holding current (don't mistake this for hooking current) is the base estimation of current that should course through the Anode along with Cathode pin of a Thyristor to keep it turned ON. In case the estimation of current reaches beneath this worth, at that point the Thyristor kills without anyone else with no outside substitution.

The SCR utilized in our circuit is TYN612 which has a most extreme holding current of 30mA (allude datasheet to know the worth), so if the present streaming however the Anode along with Cathode gets under 30mA the SCR will turn itself OFF. In this way disconnecting the force structure the heap.

The resistor R1 (0.2 ohms) and the transistor (2N2222A) assumes an indispensable job in killing the SCR. Under typical condition when the load(motor) is working, it draws current through the resistor R1. As indicated by Ohms law the voltage drop over the resistor can be determined by

Voltage across the resistor = Current through circuit x Resistor value

So as indicated by the formulae the voltage drop over the resistor is legitimately relative to the present moving across the circuits. As the present increment the voltage drop over the resistor will likewise increment, when this voltage drop surpasses the estimation of 0.7V. The transistor gets turned ON, in light of the fact that the resistor is associated legitimately over the Base and Emitter pin of the transistor. At the point when the transistor shuts the total current required for the circuit courses through the transistor immediately during which the SCR is killed since the current across it has gone beneath holding current and the voltage drop over the resistor likewise gets 0V since no current is moving through it. At last the Transistor and the SCR is killed and the Load (Motor) is likewise confined from the force supply. The total working is likewise represented utilizing the GIF picture beneath.

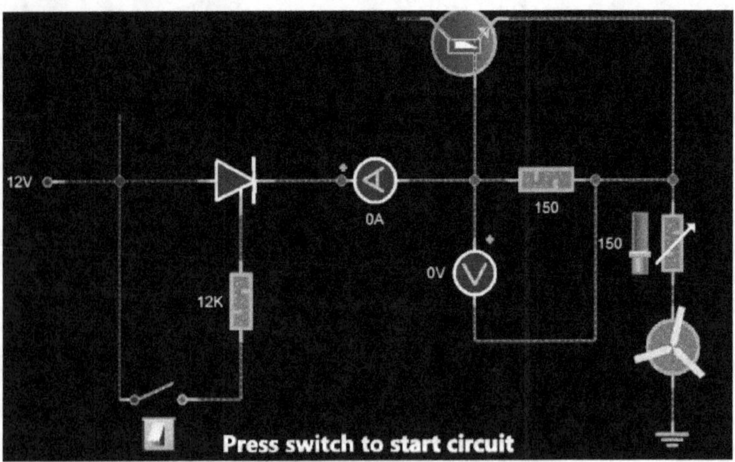

An Ammeter is set through the resistor to screen the present coursing through the Anode Cathode terminal of the SCR. This current ought not go underneath the holding current of the SCR (the holding current for the SCR in recreation is 5mA), on the off chance that it goes beneath this worth the SCR will kill. Additionally a voltmeter is set over the resistor 150 ohms to screen the voltage across it and check if the NPN transistor is being activated before the SCR closes.

Equipment:

As told before this circuit has a base number of segments, it includes one SCR, one transistor and a couple o resistors. Henceforth it tends to be effortlessly dissected by building it on a breadboard. Once more, it relies upon your application. In case you are arranging whatever is more than 2A, in this point breadboard isn't suggested. I fabricate the electronic wire circuit on a bread board and it looked something like this beneath.

As should be obvious in the picture I have utilized a LED strip as my heap, you can utilize an alternate burden or even associated your circuit which must be secured. To interface the heap to the force supply we need to press the catch which will turn on the SCR. Additionally note that I have utilized a 2W 0.2 Ohm resistor as my R2 since we need to permit an enormous estimation of current it is constantly essential to consider the wattage rating of this resistor.

Since I couldn't make a shortcoming condition by expanding the present rating I diminished the voltage to make a blame and in this manner decrease the current through the SCR. On the other hand, you can likewise short the Collector Emitter pin of the transistor with a wire this make the present course through the wire and not through the SCR and therefore the SCR will kill. After the deficiency is made and recuperated, the circuit can again be turned ON by just squeezing the catch as prior. Expectation you comprehended the circuit and delighted in learning it. In case you have any uncertainty please don't hesitate to post them on the remark segment beneath or utilize the discussions for specialized assistance.

Confinements:

Like all circuit this likewise has certain constraints with it. In case you believe that these will influence your structure, in this point you should locate another option

- The whole burden current courses across the resistor R2, consequently there is a force misfortune across it. Thus this circuit isn't fit doe battery worked applications

- The present rating for which the breaker is intended for won't be exact since every resistor will differ bit and as it gets matured the property of the resistor will likewise change.

- This circuit won't respond for unexpected spike flows since the transistor requires some an opportunity to respond to the changes.

10. STRIDE POWER GENERATION CIRCUIT UTILIZING PIEZOELECTRIC SENSOR

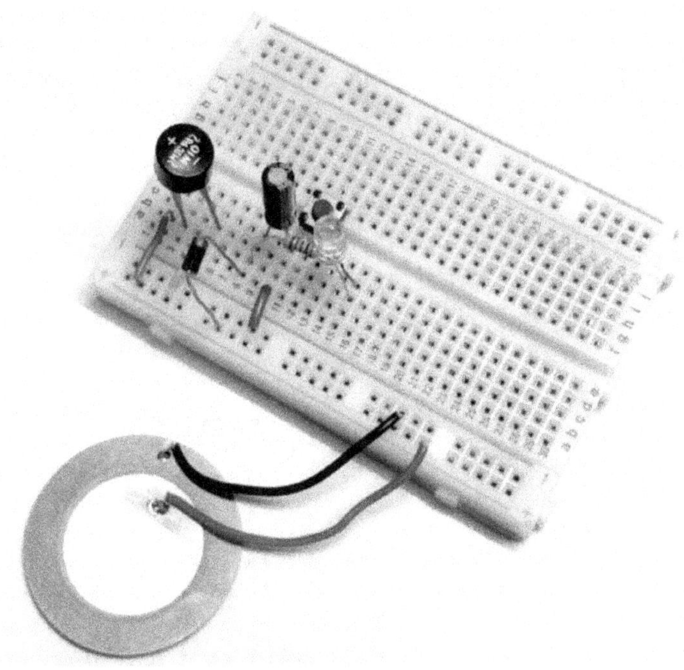

From the previous barely any years the interest of low force electronic compact gadgets expanding quickly. Because of increment in sought after of vitality utilization for the gadgets we need to thoroughly consider the option sustainable power source in human environment. In this way, it is possible that we need a durable battery or a littler force generator which utilizes human capacity to produce power and feed the gadget. For this, Piezoelectric Effect is the best guide to create power by utilizing the stride intensity of the human body.

What is Piezoelectric Effect?

Piezoelectric Effect is the capacity of some piezoelectric materials, (for example, quartz, topaz, zinc oxide and so forth.) to create an electrical charge in criticism to the mechanical pressure. 'Piezoelectric' word is gotten from the Greek word 'piezein' which intends to push, crush and press.

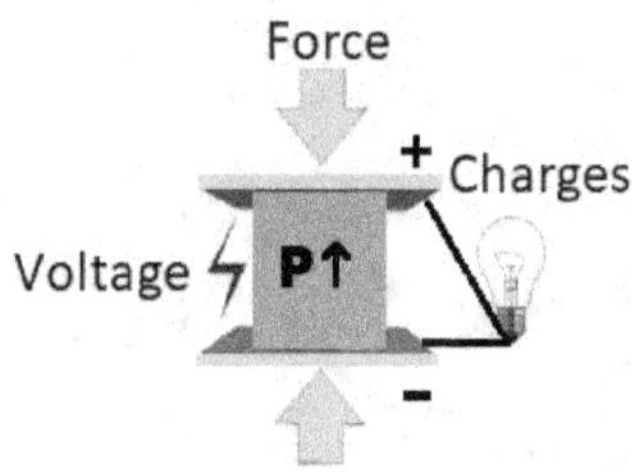

Additionally, the piezoelectric impact is reversible, which implies when we apply mechanical worry to the piezoelectric material we get some electrical charge on yield. What's more, when we apply power to the piezoelectric material, at that point it packs or stretch the piezoelectric material.

Piezoelectric impact is utilized in different application that includes

- Creation and identification of sound

- Age of high voltage

- Electronic Frequency age

- Microbalances

- Ultra-fine centering of optical congregations

- Ordinary applications like cigarette lighters

Piezoelectric Materials

Number of piezoelectric materials are accessible presently, even common and man-made. Characteristic piezoelectric materials incorporate quartz, unadulterated sweetener, Rochelle salt, topaz tourmaline and so forth. Man-made piezoelectric material incorporates barium titanate along with zirconate titanate. There are few material given in the underneath table in the classification of normal and manufactured:

Natural Piezoelectric Material	Synthetic Piezoelectric Material
Quartz (most used)	Lead zirconate titanate (PZT)
Rochelle Salt	Zinc Oxide (ZnO)

Topaz	Barium Titanate ($BaTiO_3$)
TB-1	Piezoelectric ceramics Barium titanate
TBK-3	Calcium barium titanate
Sucrose	Gallium orthophosohate ($GaPO_4$)
Tendon	Potassium niobate ($KNbO_3$)
Silk	Lead titanate ($PbTiO_3$)
Enamel	Lithium tantalite ($LiTaO_3$)
Dentin	Langasite ($La_3Ga_5SiO_{14}$)
DNA	Sodium tungstate (Na_2WO_3)

Segments Required

- Piezoelectric Sensor
- Driven (Blue)

- Diode (1N4007)

- Capacitor (47uF)

- Resistor (1k)

- Press button

- Interfacing Wires

- Breadboard

Stride Electricity Generation Circuit Diagram

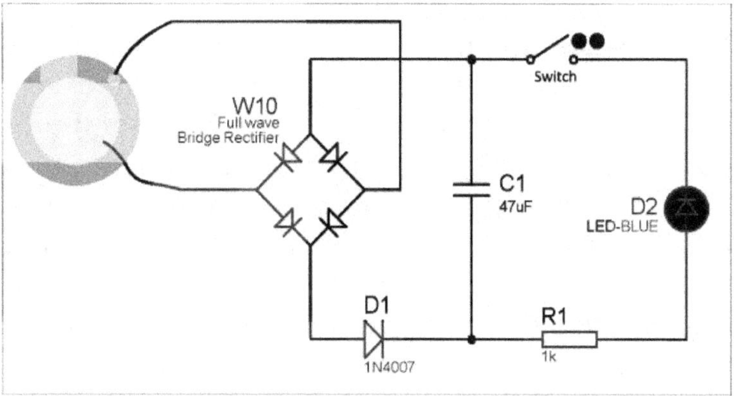

A piezoelectric sensor is comprised of piezoelectric material (quartz-generally utilized). It used to change over the mechanical worry into electrical charge. The yield of the Piezoelectric Sensor is AC. We need a full scaffold rectifier to change it into DC. The yield voltage of the sensor is under 30Vp-p, you can take care of the yield of piezoelectric sensor or can store it into battery or other stockpiling gadgets. The impedance of the piezoelectric sensor is under 500 ohm. The working and capacity temperature extend is - 20°C~+60°C and - 30°C~+70°C individually.

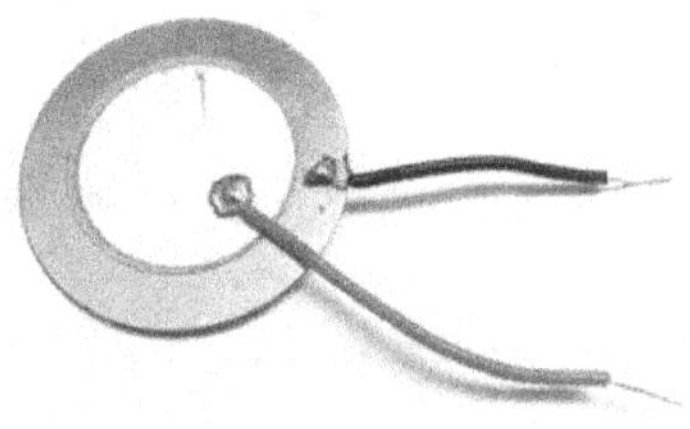

In the wake of making associations according to the Piezoelectric Sensor circuit chart, when we give mechanical worry to the piezoelectric sensor it produces voltage. The yield of the piezoelectric sensor is in AC structure. For changing over it from AC to DC we are utilizing a full extension rectifier. The yield of the rectifier is associated over a 47uF capacitor. The voltage created by the piezoelectric sensor get put away in the capacitor. What's more, when the press button is squeezed all the put away vitality is moved to the LED and LED turns ON till the capacitor get released.

In this circuit, the LED is shining for a small amount of seconds. To expand the ON time of Light Emitting Diode you can build the capacitor rating, yet it will set aside more effort to charge. Indeed, you can associate progressively piezoelectric sensor in arrangement to produce increasingly electrical vitality. Likewise, the diode is utilized for hindering the flow to spill out of capacitor to piezoelectric sensor and the resistor is flow constraining resistor. You can similarly associate a LED legitimately to the piezoelectric sensor yet it will simply streak.

11. BASIC KEYHOLE LIGHTING DEVICE CIRCUIT

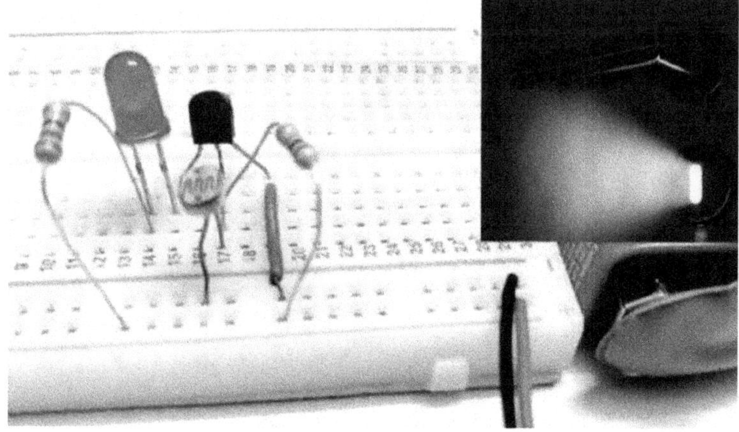

Here along with there when we arrive at home in the night it's difficult to open the entryway lock, as we can't discover the keyhole due to haziness. In this way, to dispose of this issue there are numerous keyhole lighting gadgets are accessible in the market. However, we can likewise make one effectively, utilizing LDR. Here, we are going to control the key-opening light consequently dependent on the haziness outside, the key-gap light turns ON naturally when it is dim outside and turns off when it gets splendid. It won't simply turn off or on however its brilliance will be balanced by light conditions outside.

For this Keyhole Light Circuit, we need a light sensor to recognize the light condition along with few hardware to control the Light sensor. We are utilizing a (Light Dependent Resistor) to gain power as per the force of light and transistor for exchanging.

Parts Required:

- Resistors 47K, 390ohm

- Breadboard

- Driven

- Battery 5V

- LDR

- BC547 Transistor

- Interfacing wire

Before really expounding we will initially find out about LDR and NPN transistor BC547.

Light Dependent Resistor:

LDR is Light Dependent Resistor. LDRs are produced

using semiconductor materials to empower them to have their light-delicate properties. There are numerous sorts however one material is well known and it is cadmium sulfide. These LDRs or PHOTO RESISTORS chips away at the guideline of "Photograph Conductivity". Presently what this standard says is, at whatever point light falls on the outside of the LDR (for this situation) the conductance of the component increments or as it were, the opposition of the Light Dependent Resistor falls when the light falls on the outside of the Light Dependent Resistor. This property of the decline in obstruction for the LDR is accomplished in light of the fact that it is a property of semiconductor material utilized on a superficial level. We have clarified the need of LDR in our circuit in the 'working of the undertaking' given later in the task.

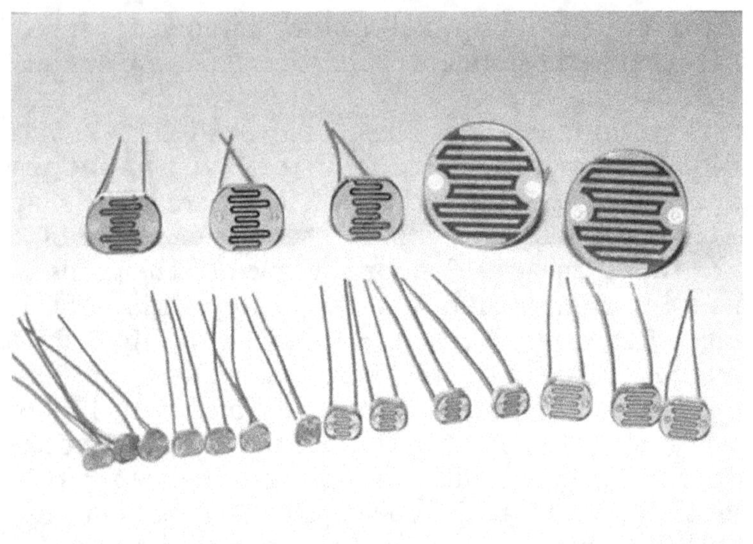

We recently made numerous Circuits utilizing LDR, which use LDR to robotize the lights as per necessity. The most well-known circuit utilizing LDR is Darkness Detector.

NPN Transistor (BC547)

Here we are utilizing NPN Transistor BC547 as a Switch. When there is no voltage given to the base of the NPN Transistor, it stays in OFF state and no present will stream among gatherer and producer, so it will go about as open switch. Presently when a little voltage (ordinarily 0.7 volt) is applied to the base of NPN transistor then it begins leading and current from gatherer to producer will begin streaming, for this situation it will go about as shut switch. Get familiar with NPN Transistors here.

BC547 permits 100mA of most extreme current course through the gatherer pin and information current breaking point is 5mA to the base pin for biasing. As the base pin kept ground the transistor moves to invert 1-sided condition and don't lead current across it (which is the Cut-Off point), as supply give to base pin it begin directing through the producer to gatherer (which is the Saturating point). The ordinary voltage go across the authority producer and base-producer is 200 and 900mV individually.

Pin No.	Pin Name	Description
1	Collector	Current flows in through collector
2	Base	Controls the biasing of transistor
3	Emitter	Current Drains out through emitter

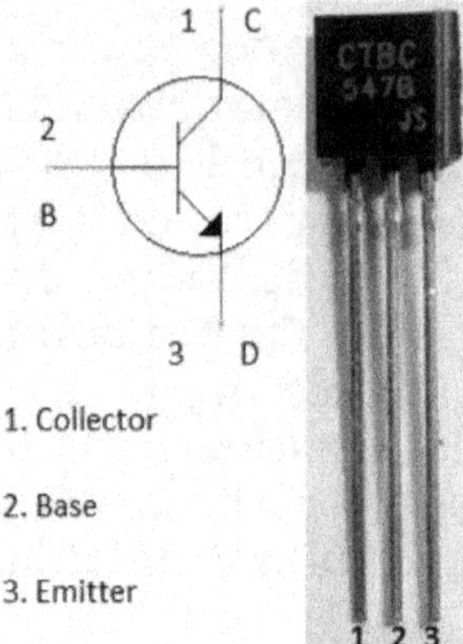

1. Collector

2. Base

3. Emitter

Negative Positive Negative transistor can likewise be used as enhancer having an addition estimation of 110 to 800. Check all the Negatice Positive Negative transistor circuits here.

CIRCUIT DIAGRAM:

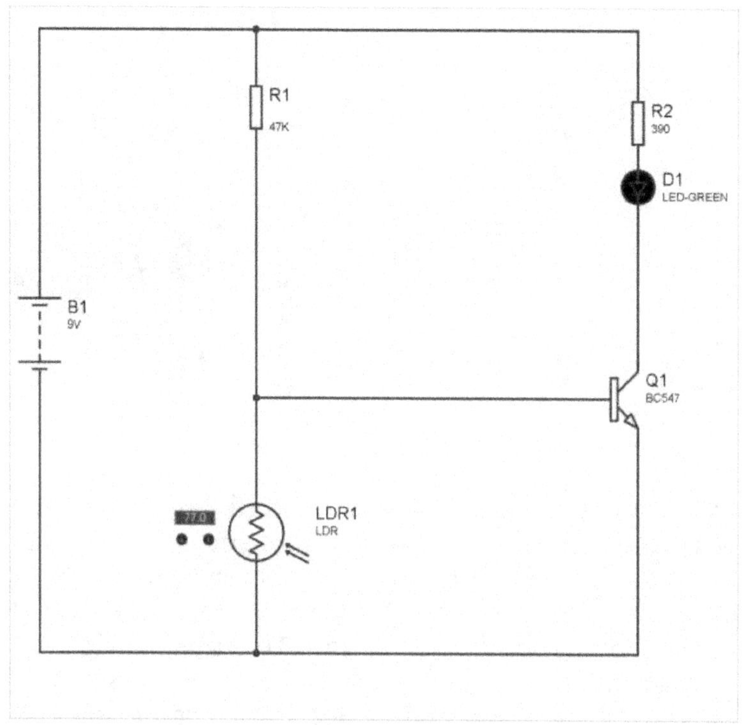

WORKING of Key-Hole Light Circuit:

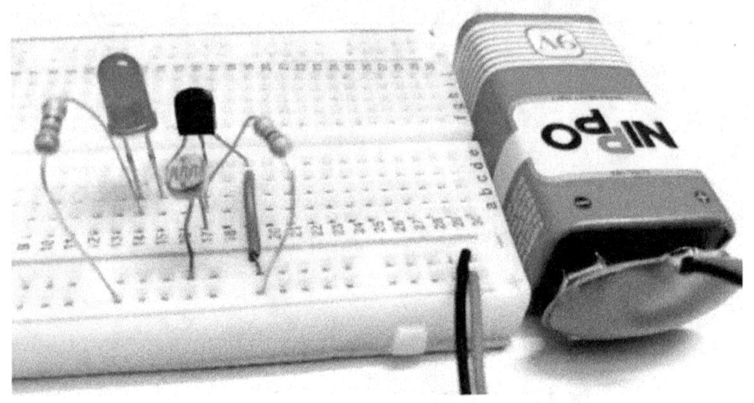

In the wake of interfacing the circuit in accordance with the circuit chart, you can fix the circuit in the key-opening in any lock. In the event that it is dull over the LDR, the opposition of LDR increments and in the event that it is brilliant LDR's obstruction diminishes. In the circuit, we are making a voltage divider circuit utilizing the 1 uber ohm obstruction and LDR and providing its yield to the base terminal of the BC547 NPN transistor.

When LDR obstruction builds (which implies dull), the base terminal of BC547 gets HIGH which permit the current to move through the authority to the producer and in this way, LED turns ON. In the event that LDR opposition diminishes (which implies splendid), the base terminal gets LOW and the LED kills.

Thus, on the off chance that we return home in night, we will discover key-opening light turned ON consequently on account of obscurity outside as well as we can without much of a stretch locate the key-gap and open the entryway.

12. BASIC TILT SENSOR SWITCH CIRCUIT

A tilt sensor is a sensor which opens along with shuts an electrical circuit when it is slanted past at certain point. It may be used in tilt counteraction gadgets, an alert circuit and in numerous DIY ventures. There are various sorts of Tilt sensor modules, for detecting the tilt the module can let loose switch or mercury switch. In this circuit, we are utilizing a Mercury-based tilt sensor.

Material Required

- Mercury Switch/Tilt Sensor
- BC547-NPN transistor
- Bell
- Driven
- Resistor - 220 ohm
- Battery 9v
- Breadboard
- Associating wires

Circuit graph

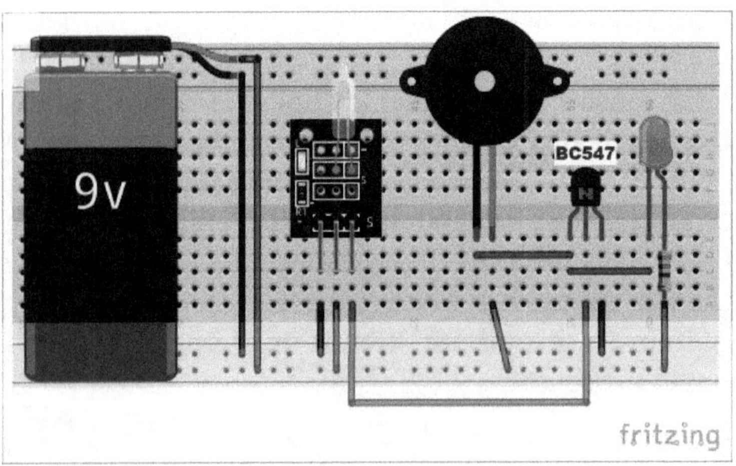

Tilt Sensor

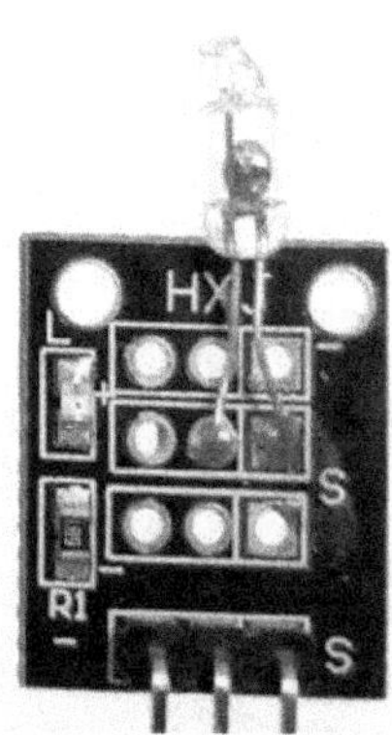

This is a Mercury switch based tilt sensor module that provides high at its yield pin when tilted. It requires a five V of Direct Current input. It's a three-terminal gadget comprise of information, ground, and yield. It has a glass tube comprise of two terminal and fluid mercury ball. The fluid mercury ball closes and opens the circuit when slanted a specific way. The working and inward structure of the module is given beneath:

Interior Structure

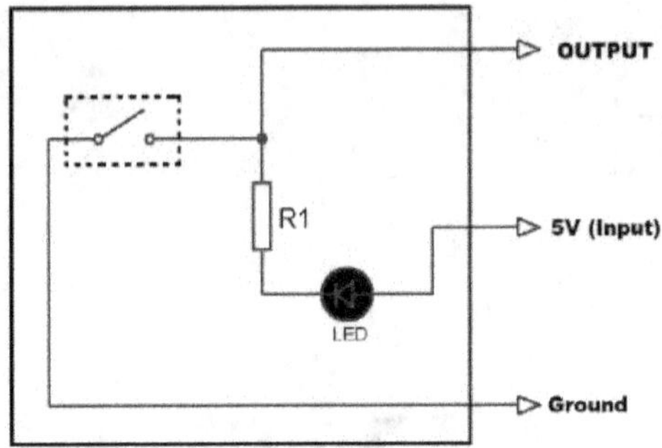

Working of Tilt Sensor

CASE 1: NOT TILTED

At first, when it is in NOT tilted situation as appeared in the picture beneath, it gives LOW yield due to the fluid mercury complete the circuit by associating the two terminals. At the point when the yield is LOW ready LED stay ON.

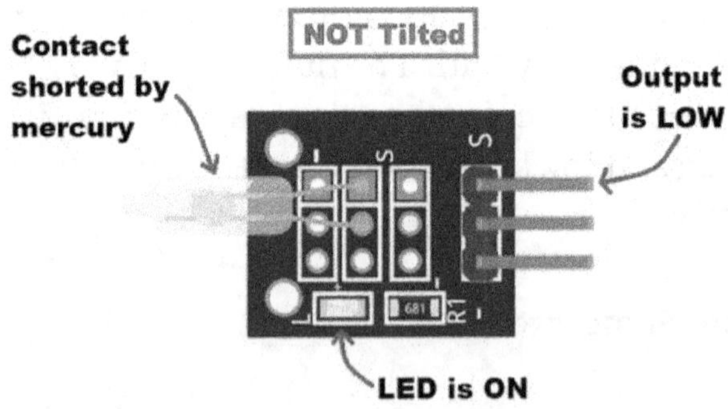

CASE 1: TILTED

At the point when it is slanted a specific way or edge, the fluid mercury breaks the contact between the metal anodes and the circuit gets open. Subsequently, we get HIGH yield in this condition and the locally available LED kills.

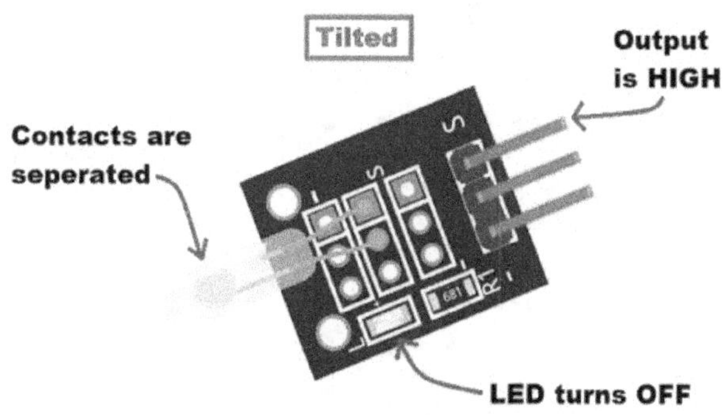

Working of Tilt Sensor Circuit:

At first, the Tilt sensor switch is in shut state which implies the yield is LOW. Presently in accordance with the circuit, the yield of the tilt sensor is feed to the base terminal of transistor BC547. At whatever point the sensor slanted to an edge or tilted the yield gets HIGH and triggers the NPN transistor into ON state. As the transistor turns ON, current through authority to producer begins streaming and the LED and Buzzer, which are associated with the gatherer terminal, turns ON.

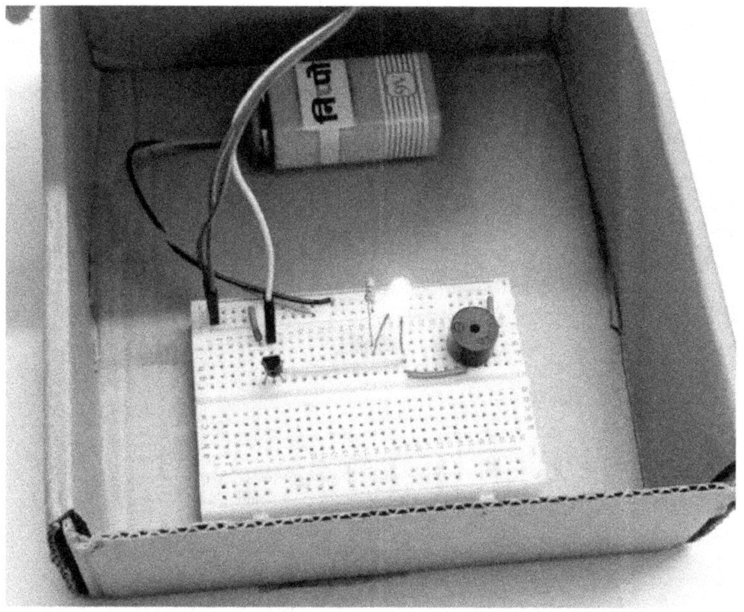

To show the tilt sensor working, we have organized a crate. The circuit is set inside the case and the Tilt sensor is put on the highest point of the container. In this way, at whatever point the container is opened, the sensor get tilted and LED and Buzzer turns ON. This can be cool side interest venture like antitheft box, caution box or mystery archive box.

13. MULTI-WIRE CABLE TESTER

In a general manner, the Cable Tester is the gadget by which we can check whether the link has absconded or it is associated in a legitimate manner. A link analyzer is the extremely valuable approach to decide the physical quality or availability of the link or wires exclusively while introducing them. It distinguishes whether the link is associated appropriately and the open quality between the parts of the bargains. Some propelled link analyzer tests the sign transmission properties like obstruction, commotion, impedance and so on. A portion of the link analyzers accessible in the market are LAN, CAT 5, CAT 6, CAT 7.

In this circuit, we are demonstrating the Multi-Wire Cable Tester by which we can watch that the wire or a link whether it is damaged or not.

MATERIAL REQUIRED

- 555 Timer IC
- Capacitors (10uf-1, 10nf-1)
- Red LED
- 4017 IC
- 9V supply
- Jumper Wires
- Resistors (10k-1, 2.2 k-2, 500 k-4,)
- Bread Board

CIRCUIT DIAGRAM

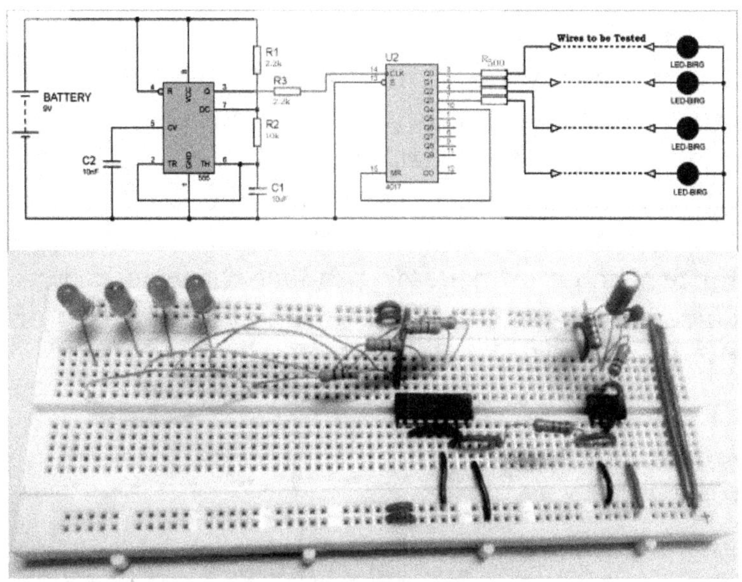

4017 DECADE COUNTER IC

As of now transferred

Here in this Cable Tester Project we have maintain 4017's clock contribution with 555 clock astable yield and associated the four wires to be tried to the four yields (Q0-Q4) of the 4017. Four LEDs are additionally associated with those four wires, which show whether wires are working or damaged. In case all the four wires are fine, at that point all the four LEDs will be squinting consistently and in case any of the wire breaks, at that point separate LED will quit flickering

Working of Cable Tester

In this circuit, we are utilizing 555 Timer IC in astable mode to create a clock signal. The recurrence of Clock beat is subject to obstruction R1 = 2.2 K?, R2 = 10 K?, and capacitor C1 = 10μF. For finding the estimation of these segments you can utilize the 555 clock recurrence number cruncher to produce the necessary recurrence. The speed of flickering LEDs will rely on this Frequency.

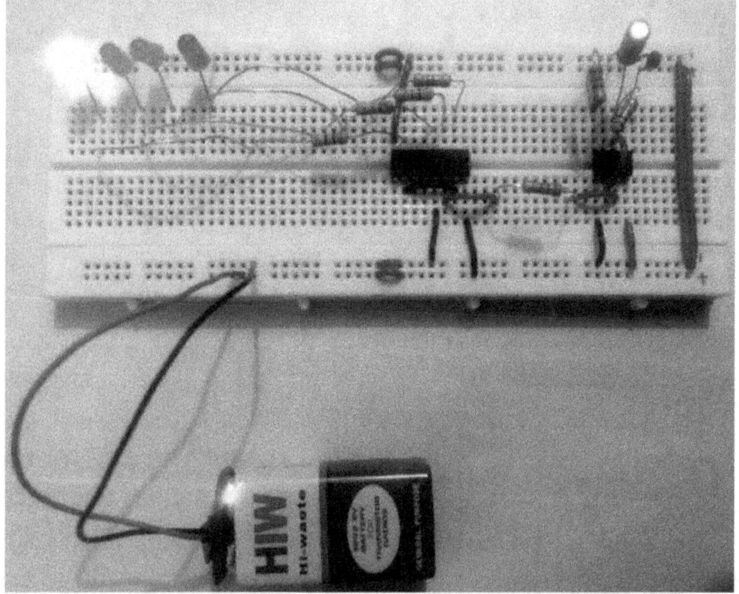

The clock beat through the 555timer IC feeds to the pin 14 of a multi decade counter IC. As we are utilizing just four yields of this IC so we have associated the fifth yield to the reset pin to reset the IC. So that when the fifth yield Q4 is high, it resets the IC and makes the

Q0 high once more.

We have utilized four wires to exhibit 4 wire Cable Tester. On the off chance that the wires are not imperfect, at that point it permits the current to lead across them and feed to the Light Emitting Diode along with the LED goes HIGH. In case there is any issue, break in the wire the LED won't gleam. By which we will become acquainted with that there is some deformity in the wire. Here, the test is finished we get the impact of wire that whether it is inadequate or not. So in case all the four wires are fine, in this point all the four LEDs will be flickering constantly and in case any of the wire breaks, at that point individual LED will quit squinting.

14. LONG RANGE IR TRANSMITTER CIRCUIT

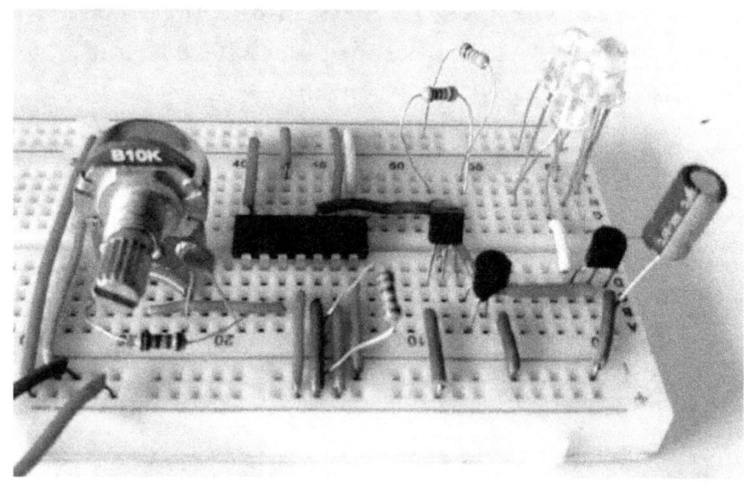

One of the most regularly utilized sensors in Electronics is IR sensor (Infrared Sensor). IR sensor helps in recognizing the warmth and the movement of an item. In the infrared range, all the items produce some type of warm radiations. These radiations are undetectable to a natural eye and must be detected or recognized by an IR sensor. An IR sensor comprises of IR Transmitter which is utilized for producing IR beams and IR Receiver (Photodiode) which is utilized for identifying that radiated IR beams. Typically, the scope of an IR radiation from an ordinary IR LED is

2~10cm with location point 35 °.

By utilizing this Circuit, we can build the scope of produced IR radiation up to 100cm. It implies we can expand the IR transmitting separation on numerous occasions utilizing this Long Range IR Transmitter circuit. Here we have utilized numerous IR LEDs to build the separation. Likewise learn here about How IR sensor functions.

Material Required

- CD4047 IC
- IR LEDs – 3
- Transistor – BC547 and BC557
- MOSFET – BS170
- Potentiometer (10k)
- Capacitor (100uF-1; 470pF-1)
- Resistor (10k-2; 2k-1; 22ohm-1)
- Bread Board
- 9v supply input
- Associating wires

Circuit Diagram

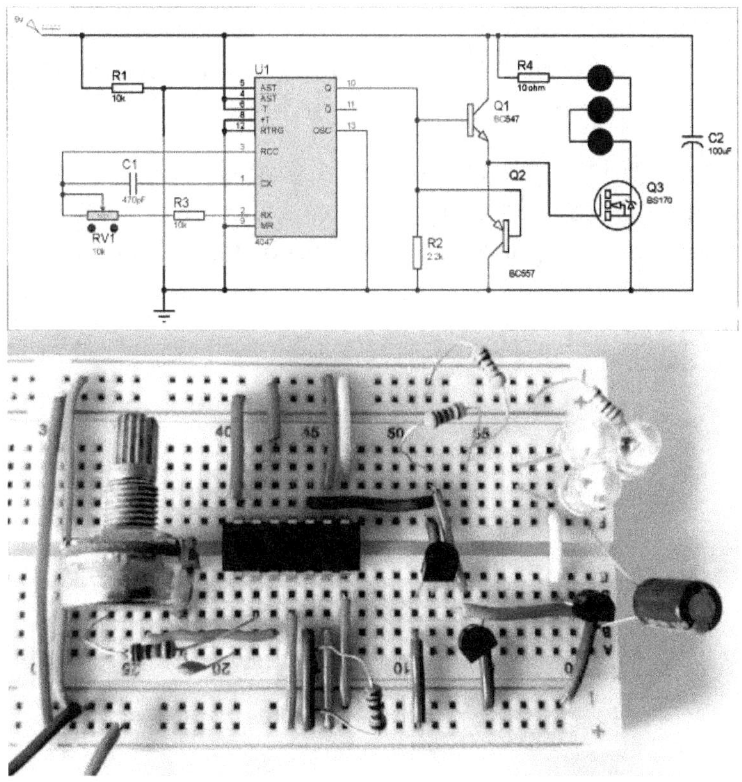

CD4047 IC

The 4047 IC is one of the mainstream IC with low force utilization. It gives both Monostable (1-shot) and Astable (free running) activity. It has a wide scope of information voltage (3v to 18v) and DC current info is up to ±10mA with a high working temperature scope of -55°C to +125°C. Here, we are utilizing this IC to create a swaying square wave yield whose recurrence will be chosen by resistor R3 and capacitor C1.

You can use the IC for producing clock beat for different applications. This IC is chiefly utilized in Inverter circuit to create Alternating current from DC current.

Use of this IC are Frequency discriminators, Timing circuits, Time-defer applications, Envelope location, Frequency augmentation, and Frequency division.

Pin Diagram

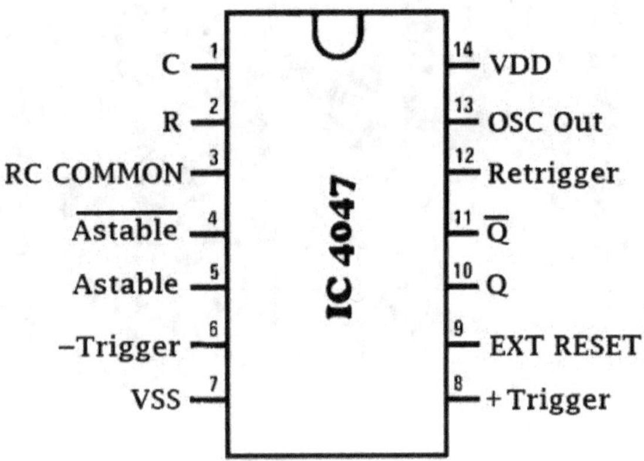

Pin arrangement IC 4047

Pin No.	Pin Name	Description
1	C	Used to connect external capacitor

2	R	Used to connect external resistor
3	RCC	Common pin for connecting resistor and capacitor to it
4	AST'(Astable bar)	Low when used in Astable mode
5	AST	High when used in Astable mode
6	-Trigger	When used in Monostable mode we give High to Low transition to this pin
7	Vss	Ground pin of IC
8	+Trigger	When used in Monostable mode we give Low to High transition to this pin
9	EXT RESET	It's an external reset pin. By giving a high pulse to this pin, it resets the output Q to low and Q' to high
10	Q	Give normal high output
11	Q'	Inverse output of pin 10,

		means it gives low output
12	Retrigger	Used in Monostable mode to simultaneously retrigger +trigger and –trigger pin
13	OSC Out	Gives oscillated output
14	Vdd	Positive input pin of IC

MOSFET BS170

These parts are intended to limit on-state opposition so as to give quick and solid exchanging execution. BS170 can be utilized in different application requiring a DC current up to 500mA. Most appropriate for low voltage and low ebb and flow applications, for example, little servo engine control, power MOSFET door drivers and for other exchanging application. The Drain-Source and Gate-Source Voltage of BS170 is 60V most extreme. The Operating and Storage Junction Temperature Ranges from-55 to +150 °C.

Pin Diagram

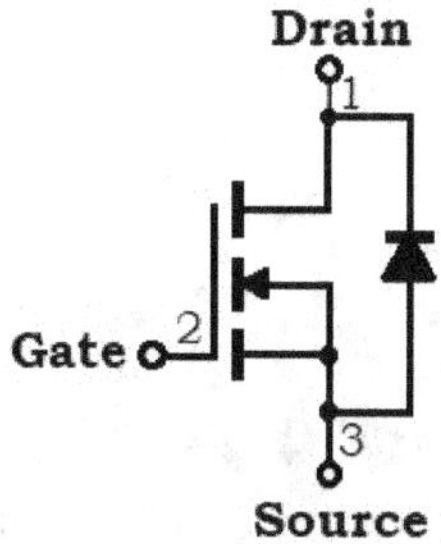

Pin Configuration

Pin No.	Pin Name	Description
1	D	Drain terminal of BS170
2	G	Gate terminal, used of turn ON the BS170
3	S	Source terminal of BS170

Working of Long Range IR Transmitter

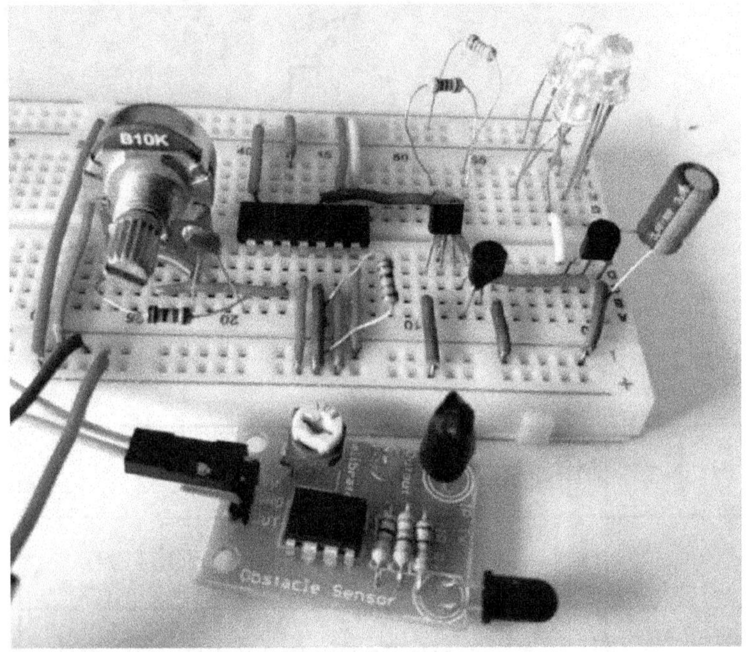

The circuit causes us to build the scope of transmitting IR beams. We have utilized three IR LEDs in arrangement for expanding the transmitted force.

A resistor along with capacitor are remotely associated with the PIN 2 and PIN1 individually, short with PIN 3 of 4047 IC. The blend of resistor and capacitor (RC) creates yield with a specific wavering recurrence. At that point this yield is taken care of to the base of both the transistor Q1 and Q2.

IC4047 is creating 38KHz recurrence, which is close to IR and RF remote control recurrence. At that point, tweaking the approaching sign or information by utilizing this recurrence wave as a bearer wave. Thus, we get a high scope of yield at this recurrence. Additionally, IC4047 is utilized to create swaying wave for transistor and MOSFET.

A MOSFET BS170 is utilized for expanding the circuit effectiveness. The MOSFET goes about as a switch and lessens the force misfortune. Force loss of transistor is high in contrast with the MOSFET, accordingly we have utilized a MOSFET rather than transistor. A 100uF capacitor is utilized to evade any plunge during killing ON/OFF. It supplies additional charge during turning ON activity.

Additionally, a Darlington pair is made utilizing NPN (BC547) and PNP (BC557) transistor for dodging twisting of the entryway drive input. As a MOSFET shows huge capacitance across door source terminals.

The three IR LEDs are associated with the Drain of the MOSFET. As the door terminal of MOSFET get signal it permits the MOSFET to lead current through Drain to Source and LEDs begin transmitting IR beams in a higher range then a typical IR LED. Subsequently, we get an IR beam of long range which is detected by an IR recipient.

15. MULTI-WAY SWITCH CIRCUIT

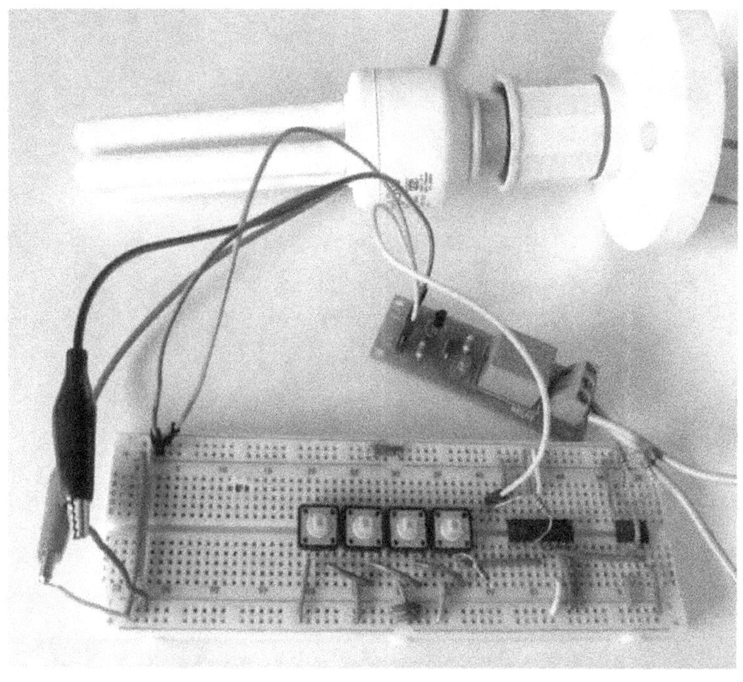

Multi-way exchanging is the most widely recognized technique to be found in the electrical framework. It gives client the solace to kill ON and any electrical apparatuses from more than one spot. The mostly recognized utilization of multi-way exchanging is for lighting frameworks and put in the most well-known zones of a structure like lobbies, banquet room, kitchen, parlor and numerous other. Multiway Switch Circuit can be effectively made by utilizing basic wires yet here we are utilizing IC CD4042. This IC can be locked at four yields by giving the clock beat, so we will control an AC light with four unique catches at four better places.

Material Required

- CD4042 IC

- NE555 clock IC

- Bulb or CFL

- Resistor (1k-2; 10k-2)

- Capacitor (0.1uf-2)

- 12v Relay driver module

- Switches-4

- 12v stock

Schematic Diagram of Multi-way Switch

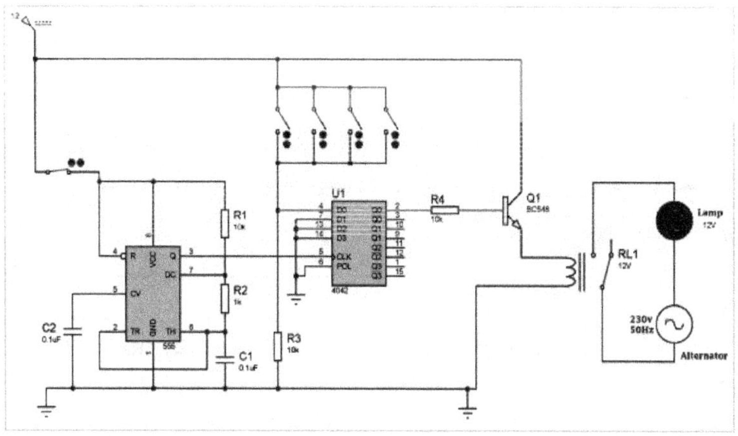

CD4042 Quad flip-flop IC

CD4042 has four flip-flop inside it, every strobe by a typical clock. It has four information input and every datum input has two yields. The stock voltage of the IC is up to 18v (max.) and DC input current is up to ±10mA. The working temperature of the IC is - 55? to 125?. The data accessible at the information input is moved to yields Q and Q' in light of the clock and extremity input.

The rationale outline and truth table of the IC is given beneath:

Clock	Polarity	Q
0	0	Input at pin D (0 or 1)

High pulse	0	Latch
1	1	Input at pin D (0 or 1)
Low pulse	1	Latch

You can comprehend the idea of utilizing the extremity by the waveform beneath:

In the event that the extremity set to Low or zero, by offering high to include, the yield waveform will rise when the clock beat get rise.

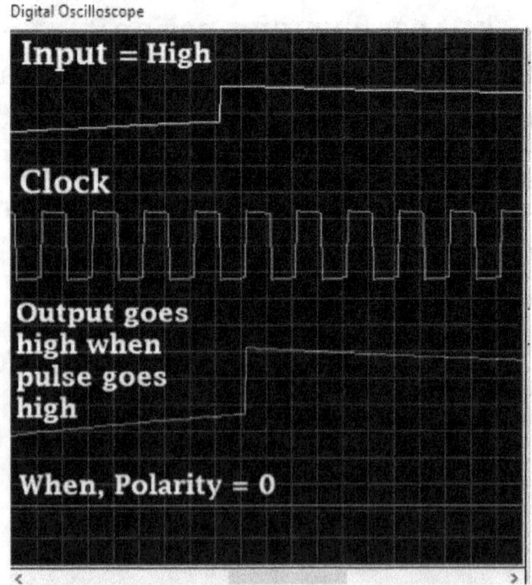

In the event that the extremity set to high or one, by offering high to include, the yield waveform will rise when the clock beat falls.

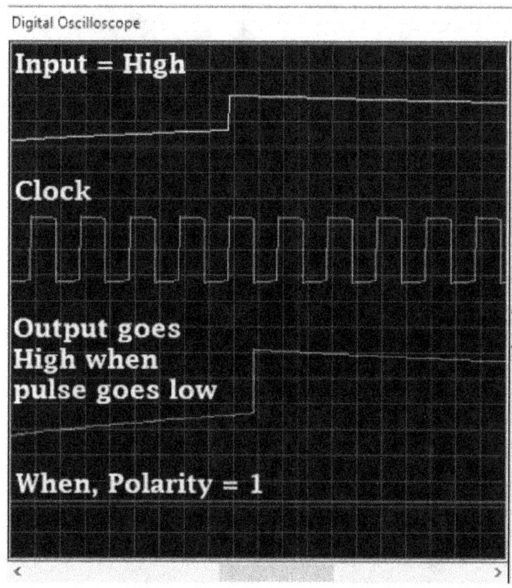

Pin Diagram of CD4042 Quad flip-flop IC

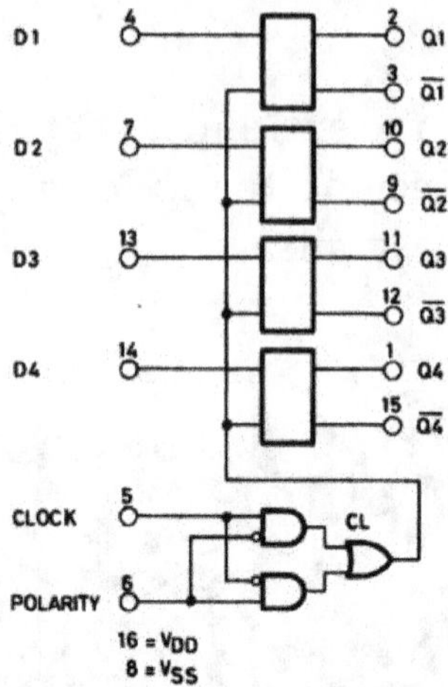

Functional Diagram of IC CD4042

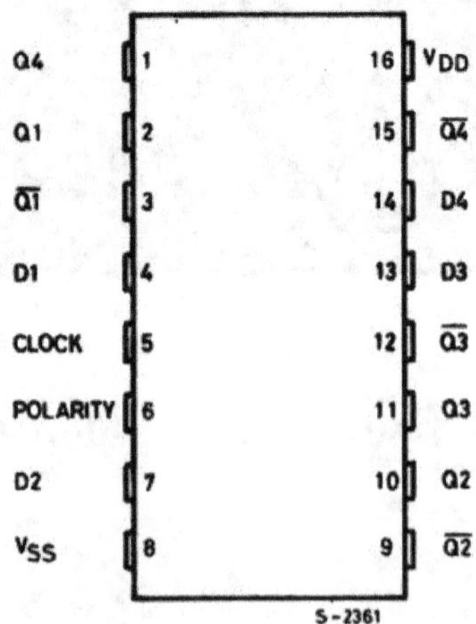

Pin Diagram of IC CD4042

Pin arrangement of CD4042 Quad flip-flop IC

Pin No.	Pin Name	Description
1	Q4	Output of D4
2	Q1	Output of D1
3	Q1'	Inverting Output of D4
4	D1	Data input of flip flop 1
5	Clock	Clock input of the IC
6	Polarity	Set to change the rise time of the Output
7	D2	Data input of flip flop 2
8	Vss	Ground Pin
9	Q2'	Inverting Output of D2
10	Q2	Output of D2
11	Q3	Output of D3

12	Q3'	Inverting Output of D3
13	D3	Data input of flip flop 3
14	D4	Data input of flip flop 4
15	Q4'	Inverting Output of D4
16	Vdd	Positive supply pin

Working of Multi-way Switch

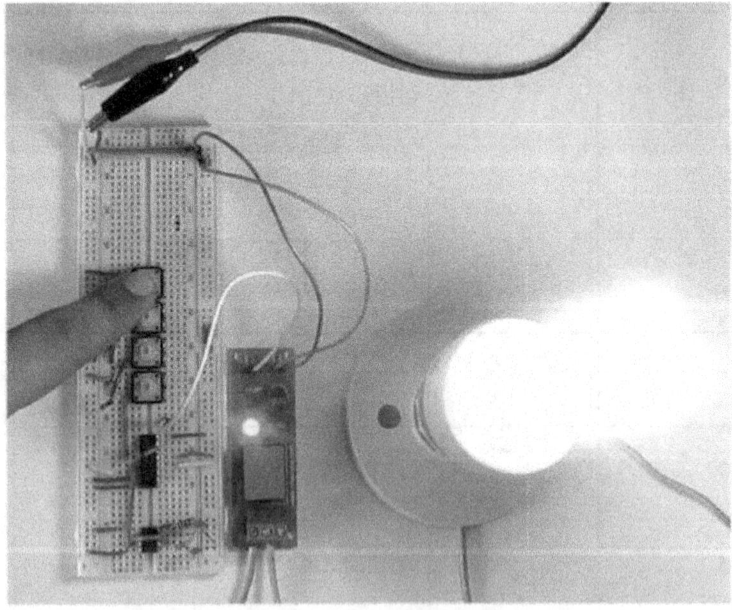

There are numerous approaches to perform Multi-way Switching. Here, in this circuit we are utilizing a CD4042 Quad flip failure IC. We are utilizing NE555 clock IC in astable mode to take care of the clock input terminal of the CD4042 IC. The flip lemon inside the CD4042 IC functions according to the table given beneath:

D	C	Q	Q'
0	Pulse	0	1
1	pulse	1	0

There are four Data pins (D0, D1, D2, D3), four yield pins (Q0, Q1, Q2, Q3) and four reversing yield pins (Q0', Q1', Q2', Q3'). From these we are utilizing information pin D0 and its yield pins Q0 and Q0', just we are utilizing just one flip lemon of the IC.

At whatever point the rationale is given to the Data pin D0 by any of the four switches, it gives yield HIGH on Q0 and LOW on Q0'. At that point a Relay module is appended to the Q0 yield pin 2. As the transfer set off the bulb or light turns ON and stay in ON state until the switch is discharged. You can turn ON the light why squeezing any of the four switches, which are determined to various area in genuine. The light will kill by discharging a similar switch squeezed for turning ON the bulb.

Rather than utilizing Push Button in the circuit you can utilize Push On and OFF catch to lock the yield in a specific state.

16. BASIC SINE WAVE GENERATOR CIRCUIT UTILIZING TRANSISTOR

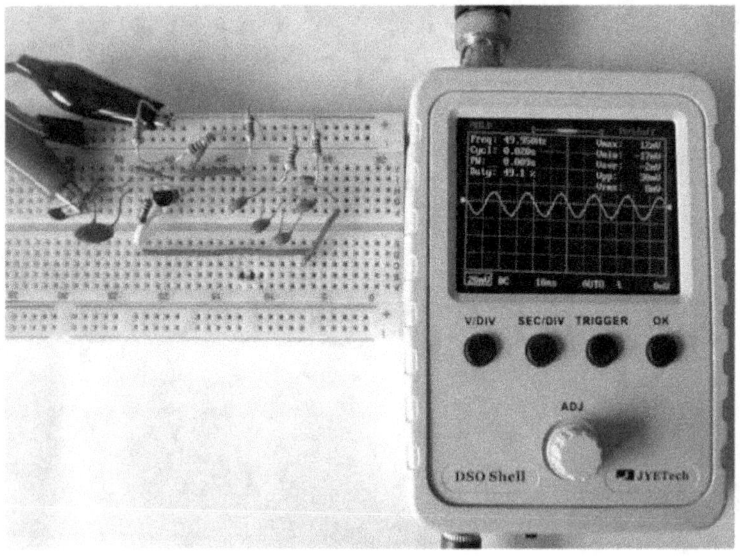

Beforehand we have fabricated straightforward Square Wave Generator circuit, today in this instructional exercise, we are demonstrating how to produce Sine wave utilizing barely any fundamental segments like transistor, resistor and capacitor. Sine wave is most ordinarily known as waveform for Alternating Current. In this circuit we will likewise fabricate that substituting waveform, we can alter the recurrence or diminish the commotion of the sine wave just by shifting the estimation of capacitors and resistors.

Segments Required

- 2N2222 NPN-transistor

- Oscilloscope

- Resistor (510, 1k, 10k, and 2k)

- Capacitors (90nf, 100nf and 200nf)

- 12v stock

- Associating wires

Circuit Diagram

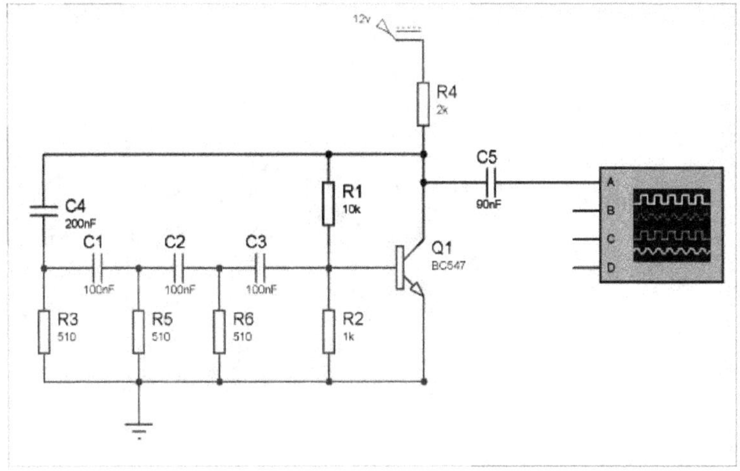

On the off chance that you see the underneath image of breadboard associations, you will discover a bigger number of capacitors than appeared in the circuit graph above. That is on the grounds that we have associated some capacitor in arrangement and corresponding to get the necessary estimations of capacitors appeared in circuit graph. You can similarly use any Negative Positive Negative-transistor rather than the over one in the circuit. Additionally you can modify the estimation of resistor and capacitor to modify the degree of recurrence.

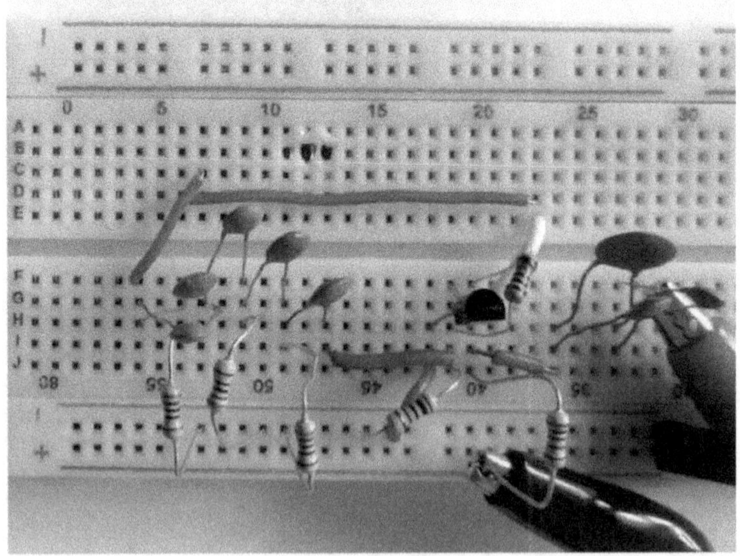

Working of Sine Wave Generator Circuit:

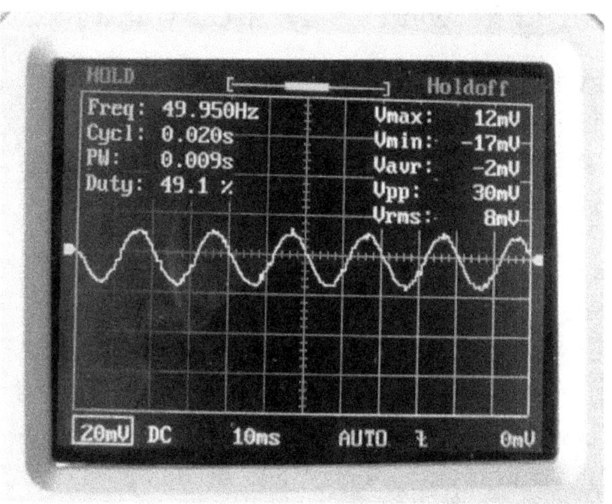

Here we are offering 12v to the circuit and we can't care of it legitimately to the transistor. In this way, for this we are utilizing resistor R1 along with R2, making a voltage divider circuit for biasing transistor Q1. We have utilized a NPN type transistor which leads the current or get forward one-sided just when a +ve sign is given to its base pin, else, it stays open or opposite one-sided.

The pair of three resistor (R3, R5, and R6) along with capacitor (C1, C2, and C3) makes a RC oscillator circuit. It's a sort of criticism oscillator which comprises of an intensifying gadget like transistor as utilized in our circuit or we can likewise utilize an operation amp.

At first, the contribution at RC circuit is DC however after the primary switch it is changed into sine wave along with afterward it stays in the sine wave.

We have utilized three capacitors, every capacitor will give 60 level of stage move. In this way, the complete stage move we get is 180 degree which a sine wave requires.

In the RC Oscillator, a portion of the yield vitality is taken care of back to its contribution, for getting positive input, positive criticism helps the abundancy of the yield to stay stable. Thus, the yield of the RC circuit is sine wave with 180 level of stage move, which is taken care of to the transistor and here the transistor is functioning as a speaker which intensifies the sine wave along with we got it at yield pin.

The capacitor C5 goes about as coupling capacitor which obstructs the DC and permits just sine wave to go through it and resistor R4 is to restrict the gatherer current.

Sine Wave Generator utilizing 4047 IC

We can likewise utilize IC 4047 to create sine wave. This IC is commonly utilized in Inverter circuit and we have recently made a Square wave generator utilizing this IC, by including not many resistors and capacitors in past circuit, we can get sine wave with IC 4047, as appeared in the circuit outline underneath:

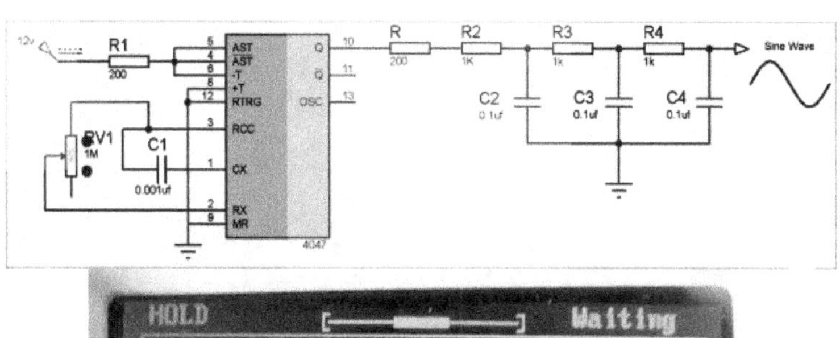

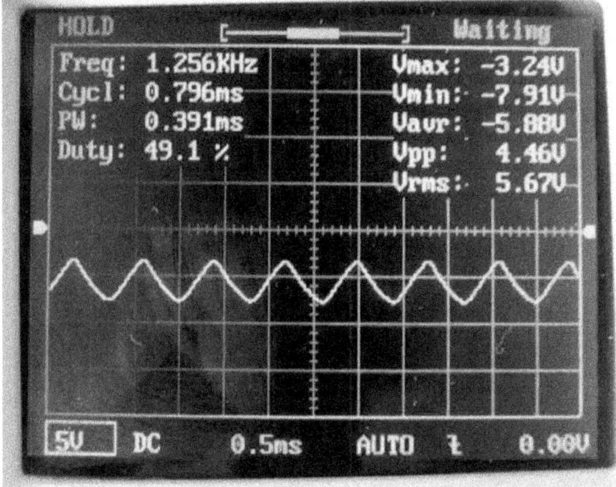

The following is that little circuit we have to include our Square wave generator to change over the square wave into a sinusoidal wave.

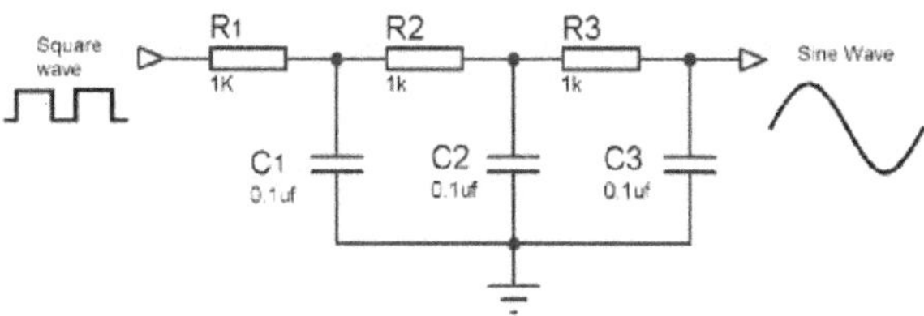

17. NI-CD BATTERY CHARGER CIRCUIT

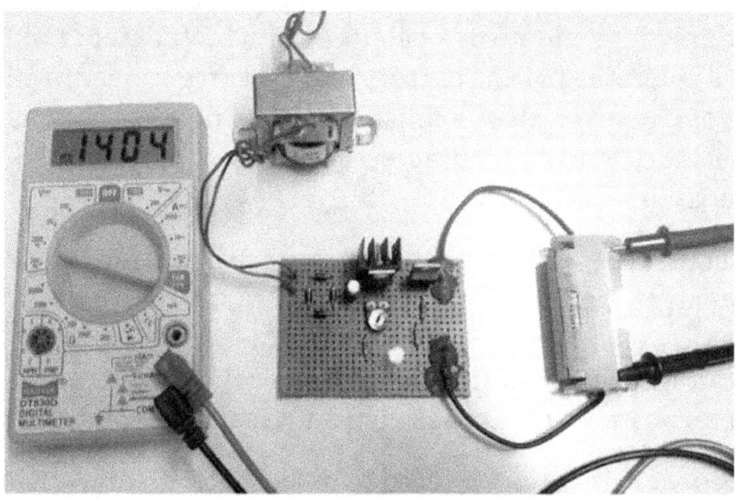

Beforehand we have constructed numerous sorts of charger circuits, that incudes Solar portable Charger, Float charger circuit, 12v Battery charger, Power bank circuit and so forth. Today we are going to manufacture charger circuit for charging Ni-Cd Battery. Towards charging Nickel cadmium batteries should be possible in two different ways:

- Quick charging

- Slow charging

The Fast charging requires an appropriate shutdown after full charge. In contrast to a Lead corrosive battery or a lithium battery, Ni-compact disc battery can't take up a buoy charge. Additionally, the shutdown of charger after full charge isn't basic. It must be done dependent on a calculation which detects the temperature of the battery and consistent decline in voltage after charge finish. Another part is that the battery must be completely released before quick charging.

Thus, here we are going to make a basic moderate charger which can charge a Ni-compact disc battery at lower and more secure flows. This procedure without auto-shutdown won't harm a cell as much when contrasted with a quick charger without auto-cut off.

Slow chargers can be used to defeat self-release. A Ni-Cd battery self-releases at a pace of 15-20% every month which is higher when contrasted with 5-10% every long stretch of a Lithium battery. In case, it is lower when contrasted with a Ni-MH battery whose self-release is 20-30% every month.

Ni-Cd Battery Charging:

The electrochemical gadget that provisions vitality to the outside circuit through an interior synthetic response is known as a Cell. A mix of these phones either in arrangement or equal association is known as a Battery.

The following is the detail sheet of not many Ni-Cd batteries of AA and AAA sizes,

Model Number	Cell Size	Top Type	Voltage (V)	Capacity mA	Standard Charge		Quick Charge	
					mA	hrs.	mA	hrs.
PS-AAA	AAA	Button	1.2	300	30	14	300	1.2*
PS-2/3AA	2/3AA	Flat	1.2	300	30	14	300	1.2*
PS-AA	AA	Flat	1.2	600	60	15	600	1.2*
PS-AAL	AA	Button	1.2	600	60	14	600	1.2*
PS-AAX	AA	Flat	1.2	700	70	15	700	1.2*
PS-850AA	AA	Flat	1.2	850	85	16	425	2.4*
PS-850AAL	AA	Button	1.2	850	85	16	425	2.4*
PS-2/3A	2/3A	Flat	1.2	600	60	14	600	1.2*

The contrast between the standard charging and fast charging depends on the charging voltage, charging current and the cut off technique or calculation.

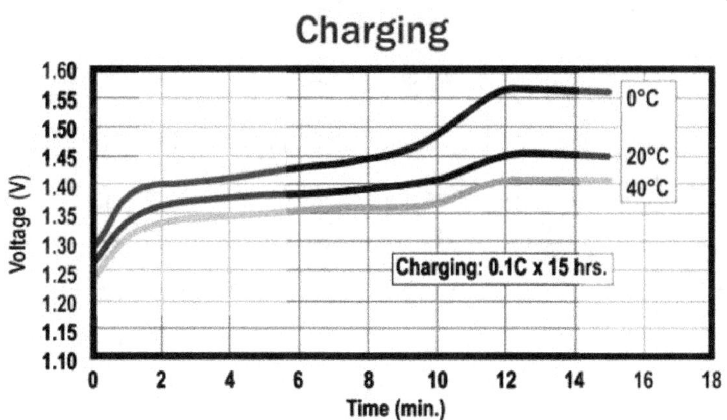

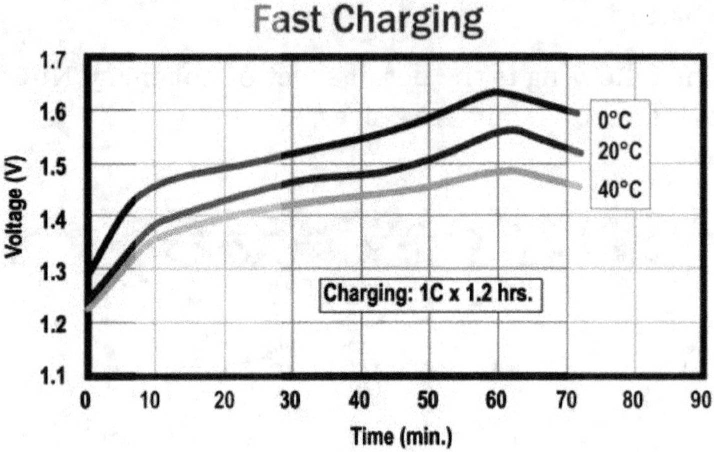

A quick charging requires exact cut off of intensity toward the finish of charge by utilizing the cell temperature or negative difference in voltage. The various sorts where the Ni-Cd battery can be charged are as underneath,

	Constant Current Slow Charge	Time Controlled Fast Charge	-ΔV Cutoff Charge	dT/dt Cutoff Charge	Trickle Charge
	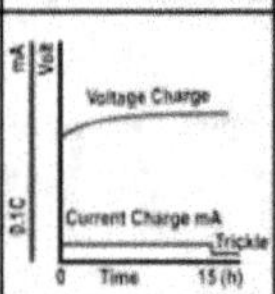	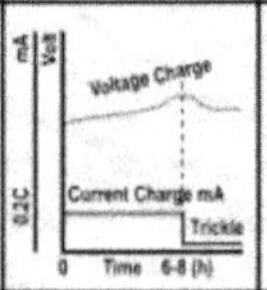	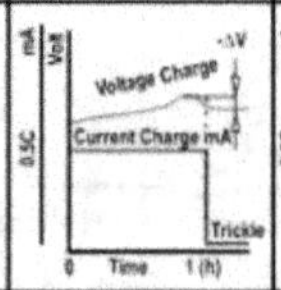	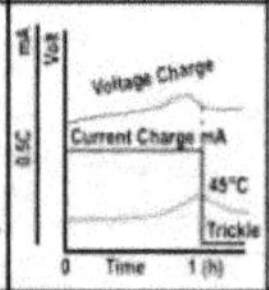	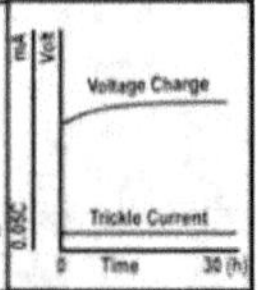
No. of output terminals	2	2	2	3	2
Charge time	15 hours	6 to 8 hours	1 to 2 hours	1 to 2 hours	30 hours or longer
Charge current	0.1 CmA	0.2 CmA	0.5 to 1 CmA	0.5 to 1 CmA	Frequent charge 1/30 to 1/20 CmA

The battery utilized here is as underneath which is of limit 600mAh and demonstrates us to charge the cell at 60mA which is 0.1C moderate charging suggested. Henceforth, we have done steady current moderate charge.

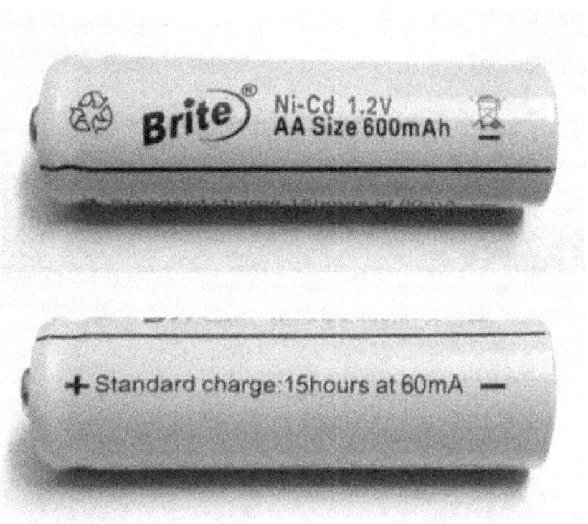

Parts Required:

- 1N4007 – 4No.

- Capacitor, 100uF (Electrolytic) – 1No.

- LM317 - 2Nos

- AAA otherwise AA battery holder – 1No

- Driven (Red - 1)

- POT (100?) - 1No.

- Resistors (1k? - 1; 560? - 1; 100? - 2)

- Interfacing wires

- Punctured Dot board

Ni-Cd Slow Charger Schematic Diagram along with Explanation:

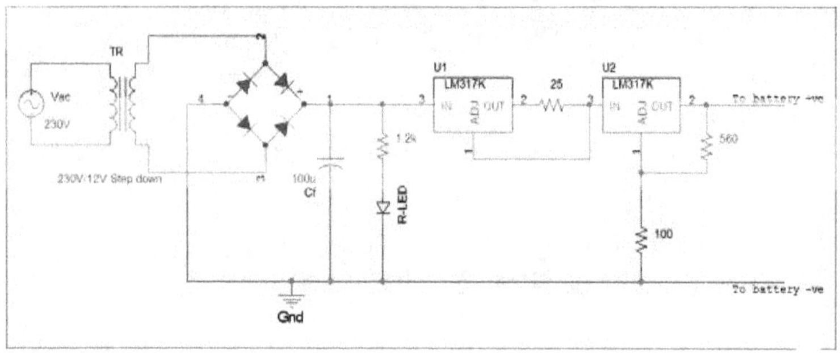

This is How the circuit looks on Perf Board:

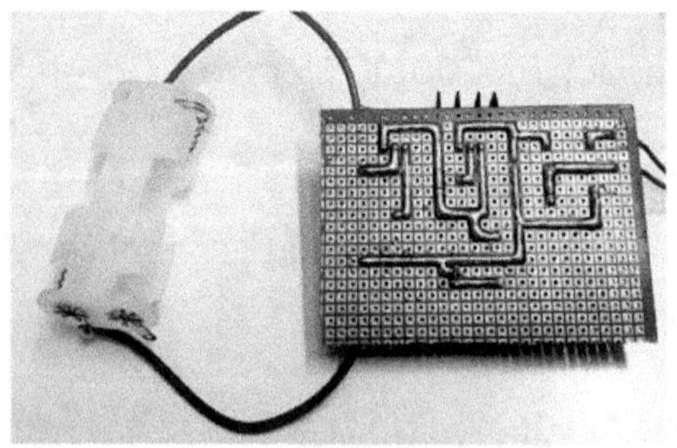

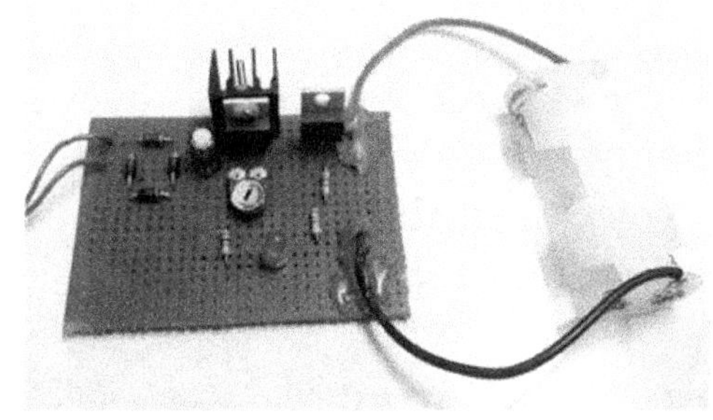

1. Venture down Transformer:

A stage down AC transformer with the rating of 230V to 15V, 1Amps is utilized here. Despite the fact that the yield current limit of transformer is at 1Amps, the admissible consistent current is just 0.4Amps for safe activity. A transformer with either 230V/0-15V otherwise 230V/15-0-15V can be utilized.

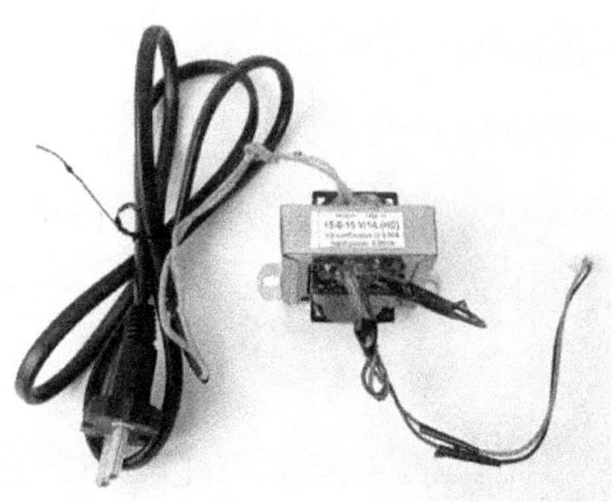

2. Extension Rectifier:

Full wave connect rectifier changes over AC supply into DC supply through a procedure called amendment and. A rectifier utilized here is finished utilizing four diodes in connect setup.

3. Voltage Regulator Circuit:

Here LM317 is utilized for voltage guideline; it is a three terminal flexible controller

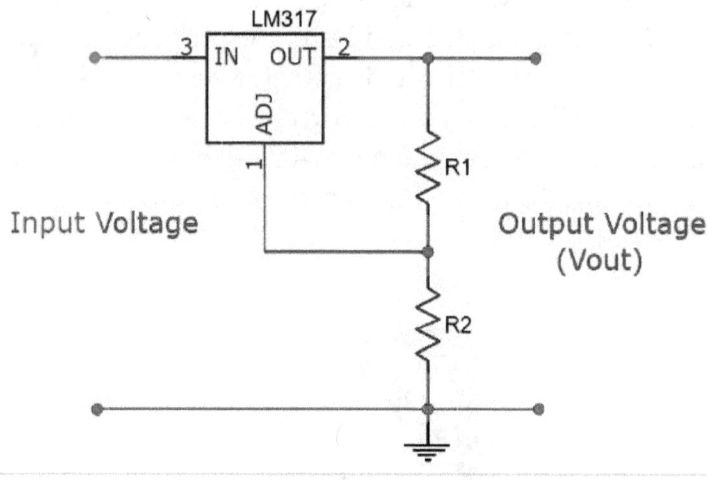

$$Vout = 1.25x(1 + \frac{R2}{R1})$$

Accordingly, the necessary yield voltage is 1.45V max to charge the battery.

VOUT = 1.25 * {1 + (100/560ohm)}

VOUT = 1.47v

This LM317 Voltage Calculator can be utilized on the off chance that you are searching for some adding machine to figure the resistor or to design the yield voltage.

4. Current Limiter Circuit:

Since the charging current for a 600mAh battery will be 60mA. The proper Resistor must be determined,

IOUT = 1.25/R

In this way, R is set to 21? to constrain the current to 0.06A.

Working of Ni-Cd Battery Charger Circuit:

The open circuit voltage without Battery shows up as 1.5v which can be viewed from the underneath picture,

As referenced before, the yield voltage is 1.49V along with the current is restricted to 60mA along with the Red Light Emitting Diode demonstrates the Charging state of the battery.

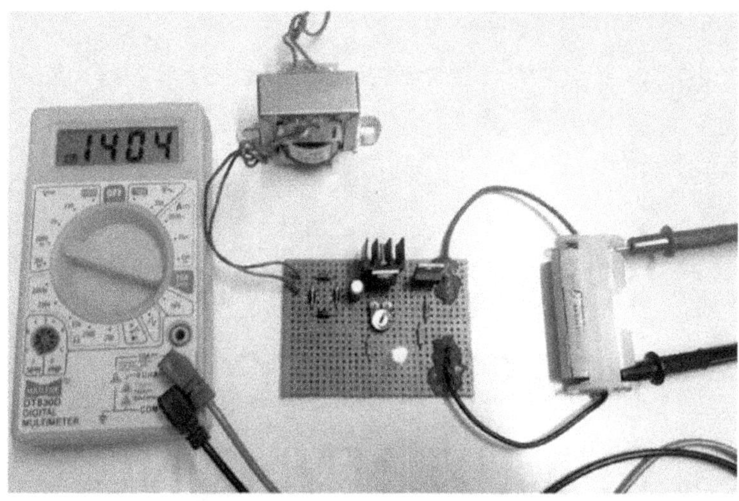

18. SQUARE WAVE GENERATOR CIRCUIT UTILIZING 4047 IC

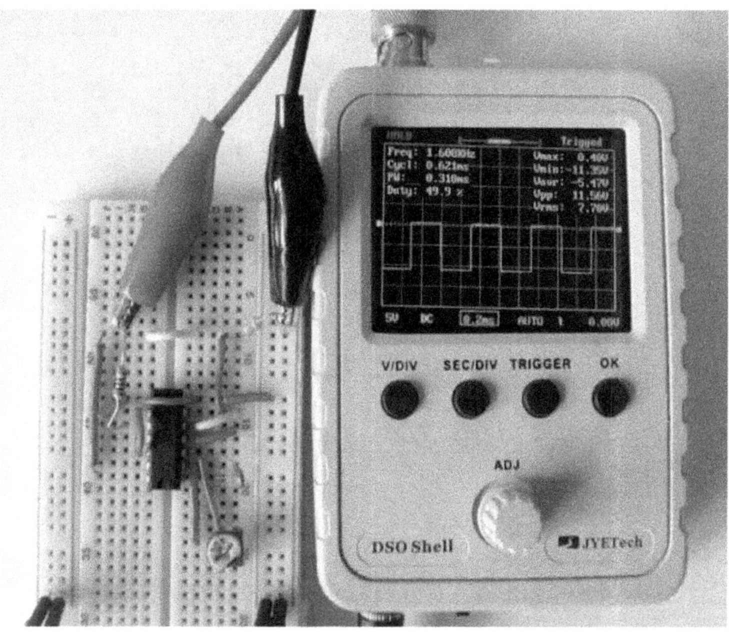

In this instructional exercise we are demonstrating that how to Generate a Low Power Square Wave Using IC 4047, we will likewise affirm the yield utilizing Oscilloscope. In the Astable mode the yield waveform of 4047 IC changes among high along with low rationale levels which is indistinguishable from the square wave. It just requires barely any resistors along with capacitors to add remotely to create the square wave. This can be utilized as a clock beat for a portion of the ICs which need clock heartbeat to work. This Square wave can be additionally changed over into Sine wave by including hardly any more resistors along with capacitors.

Material Required

- IC 4047

- Oscilloscope

- Potentiometer esteem (1M ohms)

- Resistor esteem (1k and 200 ohm)

- Capacitor esteem (0.001uf and 0.1uf)

- Interfacing wires and tests

- 12v inventory

Circuit Diagram

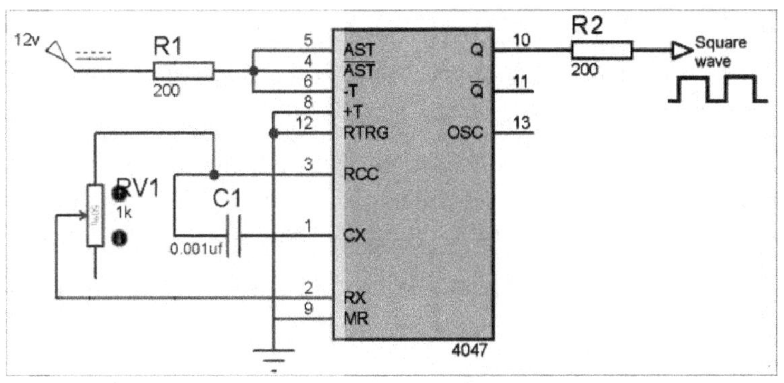

The circuit is for this Square wave generator is given previously. You can fluctuate the recurrence of square wave by moving the potentiometer or you can utilize diverse estimation of resistor along with capacitor to shift the yield recurrence.

Note: Minimum Value of R: 10 Kilo O

Most extreme Value of R: 1 Mega O

Least Value of C for Astable Mode: 100 pF

Least Value of C for Monostable Mode: 1000 pF

Before really expounding we should think about IC 4047.

IC 4047

The 4047 IC is one of the famous IC with low force utilization. It gives both Monostable (1-shot) and Astable (free running) activity. It has a wide scope of info voltage (3v to 18v) and DC current information is up to ±10mA with a high working temperature scope of -55°C to +125°C. Here, we are utilizing the IC to create square and sine wave, for this we simply need barely any resistor and capacitor. You can use the IC for producing clock beat for different applications. This IC is principally utilized in Inverter circuit to create Alternating current from DC current.

Utilization of this IC are Frequency discriminators, Timing circuits, Time-postpone applications, Envelope discovery, Frequency increase, and Frequency division.

Pin Diagram IC 4047

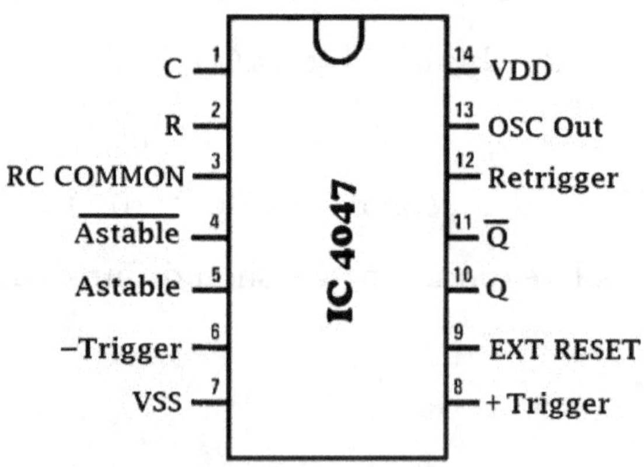

Pin design IC 4047

Pin No.	Pin Name	Description
1	C	Used to connect external capacitor
2	R	Used to connect external resistor
3	RCC	Common pin for connecting resistor and capacitor to it
4	AST'(Astable bar)	Low when used in Astable mode
5	AST	High when used in Astable mode
6	-Trigger	When used in Monostable mode we give High to Low transition to this pin
7	Vss	Ground pin of IC
8	+Trigger	When used in Monostable mode we give Low to High transition to this pin
9	EXT RESET	It's an external reset pin. By giving a high pulse to

		this pin, it resets the output Q to low and Q' to high
10	Q	Give normal high output
11	Q'	Inverse output of pin 10, means it gives low output
12	Retrigger	Used in Monostable mode to simultaneously retrigger +trigger and –trigger pin
13	OSC Out	Gives oscillated output
14	Vdd	Positive input pin of IC

Working of the Circuit for Generating Square Wave

We can supply an info voltage scope of 3v to 15v to the IC. In our circuit, we are giving 12v. A resistor along with capacitor is remotely combined with the PIN 2 and made short with PIN 3. The mix of resistor and capacitor (RC) creates yield with a specific recurrence. The yield for the square wave is taken from the PIN 10 in arrangement with a 200 ohm resistor.

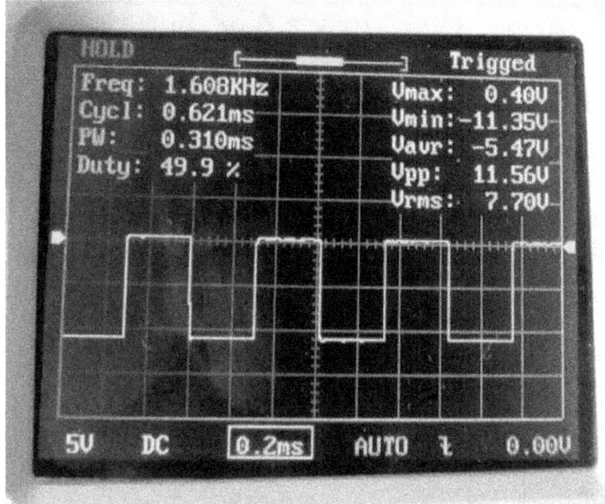

The recipe for finding the estimation of recurrence of Square Wave is given beneath:

f = 1/8.8RC

Model: for computing recurrence scientifically for the waveform appeared in figure

Here, the potentiometer is at approx. 7-8% and the estimation of C is 0.001uf.

Along these lines, the recurrence is: f = 1/8.8*70,000*0.001*10-6

f = 1623.37 or 1.6Khz (approx.)

A similar recipe can be utilized to discover the estimation of RC if recurrence is known.

The hindrance of 4047 IC is that, we can't modify the

obligation cycle and the yield of this IC has the consistent obligation pattern of half. What's more, for controlling the recurrence we use to shift the estimations of R and C in the circuit.

The square wave created by this circuit can be handily changed over into Sine wave utilizing not many resistors and capacitors.

Square to Sine Wave Converter

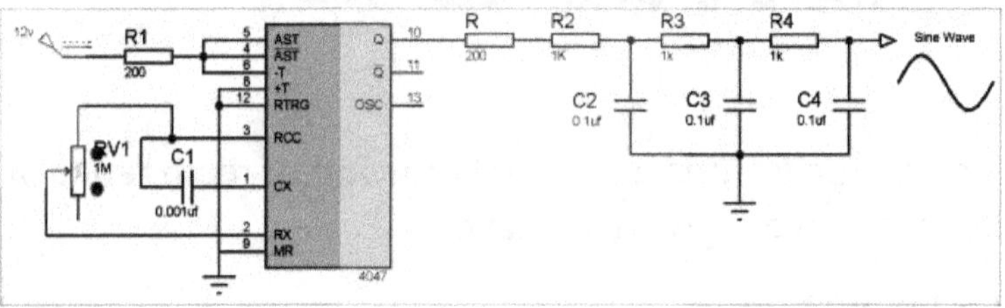

This Circuit is the adjustment of the above circuit for getting the Sine wave from square wave. For changing over the square wave into sine wave we have to include not many resistors and capacitors as appeared in the circuit graph beneath:

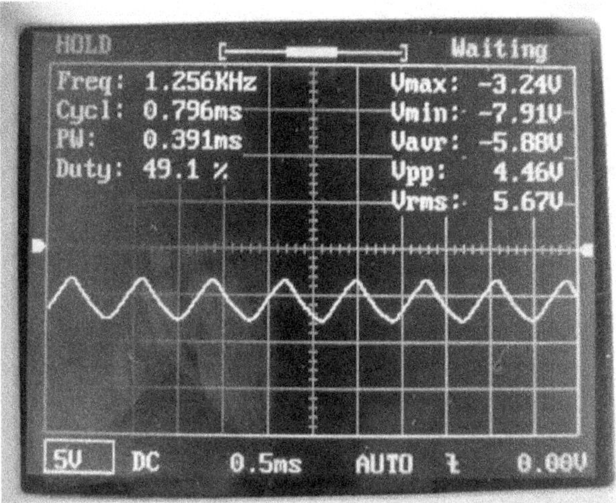

By making this little change we can change over the square wave into a sinusoidal wave.

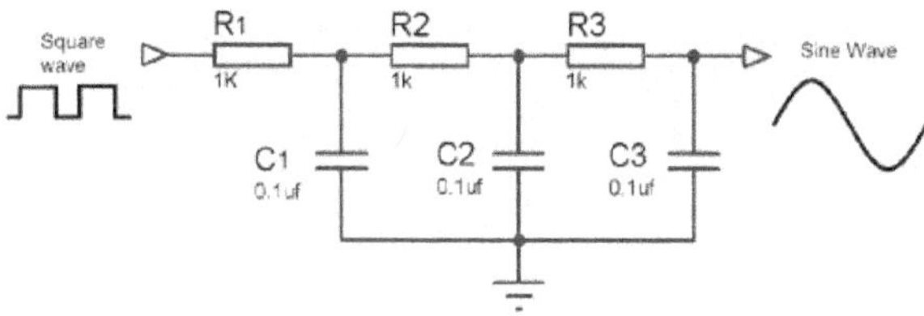

19. LM723 VOLTAGE REGULATOR CIRCUIT

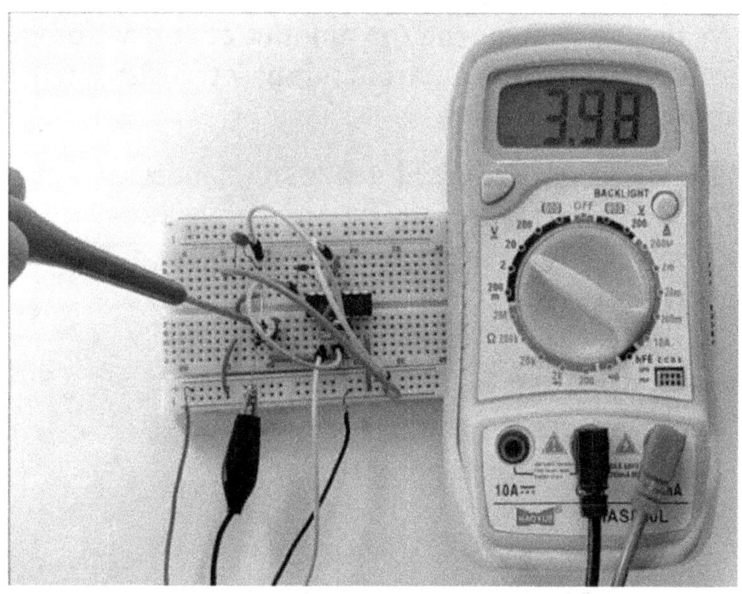

To get a directed force supply we utilize different voltage controller ICs like 7805, 7812 and so on however they all give fixed estimation of yield. For variable voltage guideline we previously secured LM317 voltage controller circuit. Today we are making Voltage Regulation Circuit utilizing LM723. This is one of the well known IC utilized for the Voltage guideline.

For this voltage controller circuit utilizing LM723 IC,

we simply need to include scarcely any resistors and capacitors with the IC according to the circuit chart given underneath. By giving 9v input power supply, we will have the option to change the controlled stock from 4v to 8v by utilizing the potentiometer in the circuit. The advantage of utilizing this IC is that it can give an over the top amount of current of up to 10A, by associating an outside pass transistor with appropriate hardware.

The stock voltage of the LM723IC is most extreme 40v and the yield ranges from 3v to 37v with a 150mA of yield current without utilizing an outside pass transistor.

Material Required

- LM723 voltage controller IC

- Resistor-10k

- Capacitor (100pf, 0.1uf)

- Potentiometer-10k

- Interfacing wires

- Battery 9v

Circuit Diagram

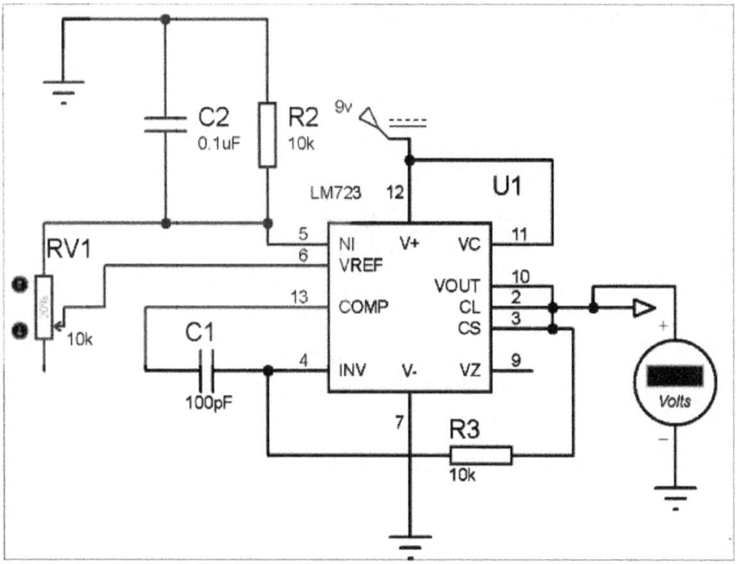

You can get the estimation of obstruction R3 by the recipe given in the datasheet of the IC LM723:

R3 = (R1*R2)/(R1+R2)

Note: This circuit is just for getting yield voltage ranges from 2v to 7v most extreme.

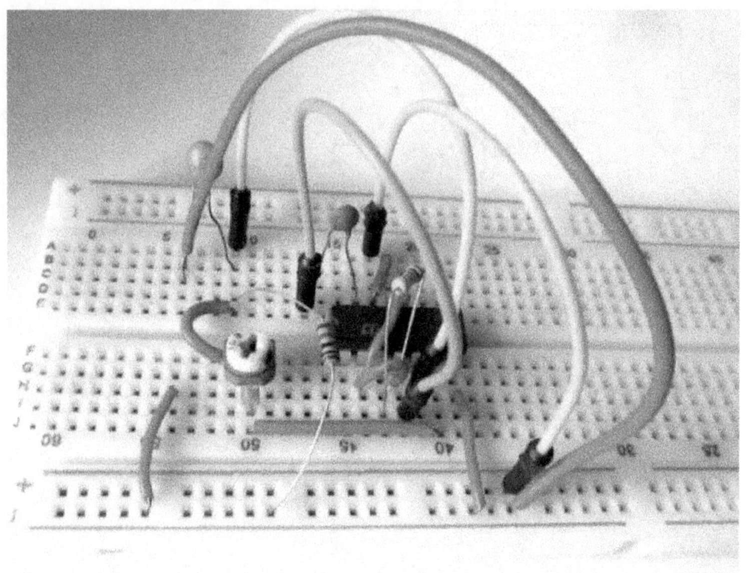

Voltage Regulator IC LM723

The LM723 is the customizable voltage controller IC intended for arrangement controller application, with a present yield of 150mA without outside pass transistor. On the off chance that we utilize a transistor remotely, it can ready to give up to 10A of current to drive any ideal burden up to this range. The info supply is 40v most extreme and its yield voltage ranges from 3v to 40v. The IC is additionally utilized in different applications like shunt controller, current controller. The IC having low backup current channel, which permit us to utilize the IC as straight or crease back current restricting, with a working temperature ranges from - 55 °C to 150 °C.

Pin chart of LM723

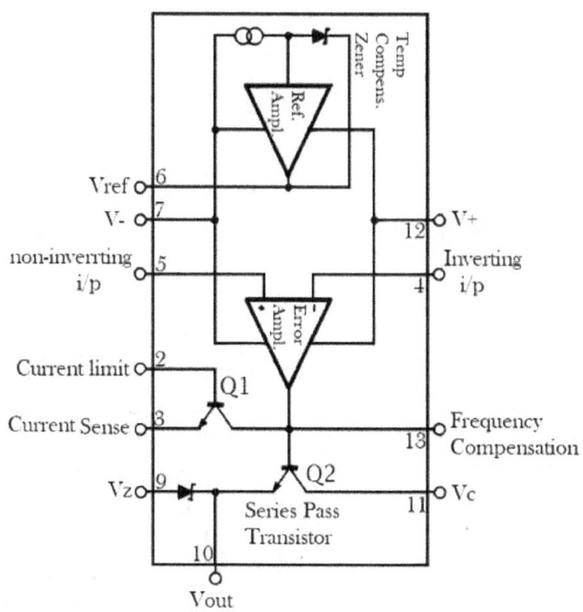

Pin arrangement of LM723

Pin No.	Pin Name	Description
1	NC	Not connected
2	Current Limit	This is the base pin of current limiting transistor Q1, used for current limiting and to reduce the power

		dissipation at fault condition to reduce the risk of heating.
3	Current Sense	This is the emitter pin of the current limiting transistor Q1, used for current limiting and fold-back application.
4	Inverting i/p	This terminal is connected to the inverting pin of the error op-amp whose output is connected to Q2 transistor, helps in providing constant output voltage
5	Non-inverting i/p	This terminal is connected to the non-inverting pin of the error op-amp, used to provide reference voltage to the op-amp.
6	Vref	It is the reference output voltage of the IC, approx. 7.15v
7	-Vcc	Ground pin of IC
8	NC	Not connected

9	Vz	Connected with the anode terminal of the Zener diode and cathode of Zener diode is connected to Vout, it is generally used for making negative voltage regulators
10	Vout	This terminal provides an output voltage range from 3v to 37v with a current rating of 150mA.
11	Vc	Connected with collector input of series pass transistor. Supplied directly through source when not connected with the series pass transistor.
12	V+	Positive supply of IC
13	Frequency Compensation	This terminal is used for connecting a capacitor with inverting input of the IC to reduce the noise. As per internal connection it is the output pin of error amplifier. Typically the value of capacitor is 100pf or

		you can use datasheet for the same.
14	NC	Not connected

Working of LM723 Voltage Regulator Circuit:

A voltage of 9v is given to the reference enhancer through V+ (PIN 12) of LM723 to get a steady yield voltage at Vref Pin 6. The reference voltage is then moved to the non-reversing Pin 5 of the IC by interfacing potentiometer and capacitor with it. The voltage at the non-reversing pin is utilized to contrast and rearranging pin voltage. In the event that the voltage at non-transforming input more prominent than reversing pin, at that point the arrangement pass transistor get forward one-sided and permit the current to move through the gatherer to producer and we get the yield voltage through PIN 10. In this circuit, we are utilizing potentiometer RV1 rather than R1. We can modify the voltage in accordance with the necessity by moving the potentiometer RV1.

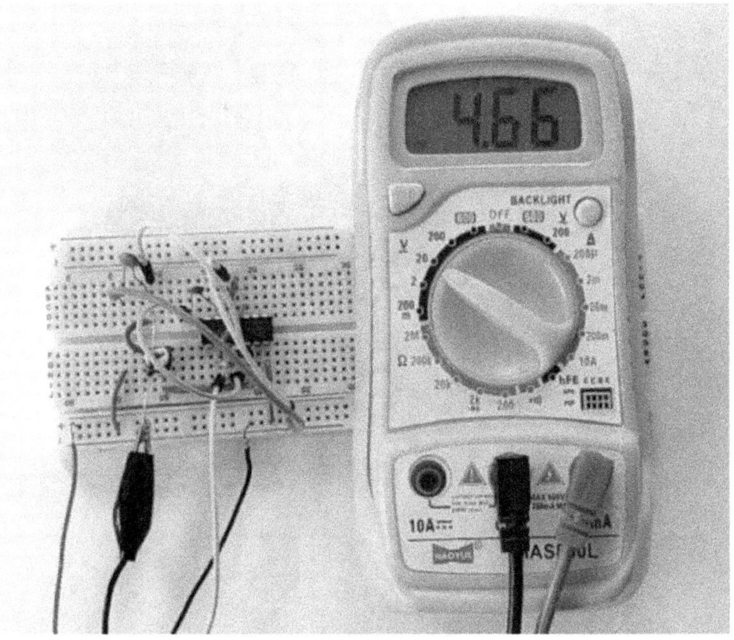

The equation for finding the yield voltage of this circuit, as per Voltage Divider Rule, is:

Vout = Vref*(R2/RV1+R2)

The greatest yield can be created by this circuit is 7v and least is 2v, for getting higher or lower than this scope of yield voltage, there are many circuits graphs presents in datasheet which gives the diverse scope of yield voltage to be required.

20. BASIC LIE DETECTOR CIRCUIT UTILIZING TRANSISTORS

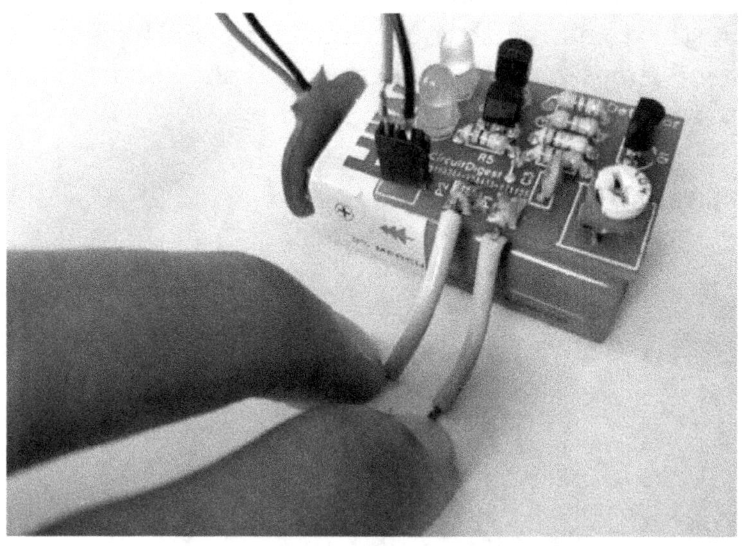

Gadgets has a ton of fun to play with, when we gain proficiency with the very rudiments of how every part functions along with how to use them in our circuit it's genuinely simple to configuration, reenact and create our thoughts into a PCB. In this venture we should construct a basic fun circuit, break down it and afterward manufacture a PCB to improve our expectation to absorb information. The idea driving this Lie Detector Circuit is that, we expect when an individual untruth he sort of siphons up his uneasiness level which makes him perspire and create dampness on his skin. We at that point utilize this bit of circuit to identify if there is dampness on his skin and dependent on the outcome we sparkle and LED, a green one for truth and red for lie. Obviously yes this can't be asserted as an untruth finder, yet you can utilize this to play with your companions and have some good times. More than that you get the opportunity to learn stuff. So Let's begin...

Materials Required:

- Bread board

- BC547 Transistor (3 Nos)

- Driven (2 Nos)

- Capacitor (100nF)

- Resistors (1M, 10K, 470, 47K)

- Potentiometer (50K or 100K)

- Associating wires

Schematic Diagram along with Explanation:

We should not hop into the circuit graph straight away. Allow yourself a moment to think how this Lie Detector Circuit would really be. So we have two LED's which must be turned on or killed dependent on the obstruction estimated (it's connected with dampness) between two finger. In what manner can we really go with this?

Since we are exchanging LED clearly we need transistors and estimation of resistor estimated between two fingers won't differ much concerning dampness so we need an intensifier which could likewise be made utilizing a transistor. Enough pieces of information! give something a shot your own and afterward investigate the circuit outline underneath:

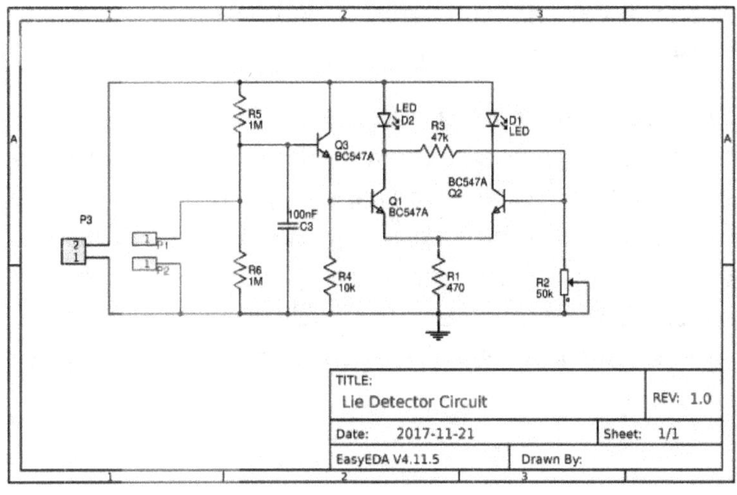

This is the circuit that we are going to utilize. The connector P3 is for supply voltage (2 is +9V and 1 is ground). The cushions P1 and P2 are where you require to put your fingers. Presently we should break down this to know how it functions.

On the off chance that you investigate you can find that the transistor Q3 along with Q1 chooses the status of LED D2 and the transistor Q2 chooses the status of LED D1. The Resistor R5 and R6 structure a potential divider where the estimation of R6 is exposed to change since it has the cushions P1 and P2 across it. So at whatever point the fingers are put the estimation of R6 will differ. This variety influences the base voltage of the transistor Q3. The transistors Q3 along with Q1 are associated as a Darlington pair consequently little variety of base voltage Q3 will influence Q1. Henceforth dependent on the opposition of the finger the transistor Q1 and Q3 will conclude either to kill on or turn the LED D2.

The Light Emitting Diode D2 will turn on just if the Transistor Q1 is on, however when this transistor goes on the voltage to the base of Q2 transistor will be low along these lines keeping the LED D1 killed. The base voltage of the transistor Q2 can be constrained by the Potentiometer (50K). Along these lines, you can use this potentiometer to set the affectability of the circuit.

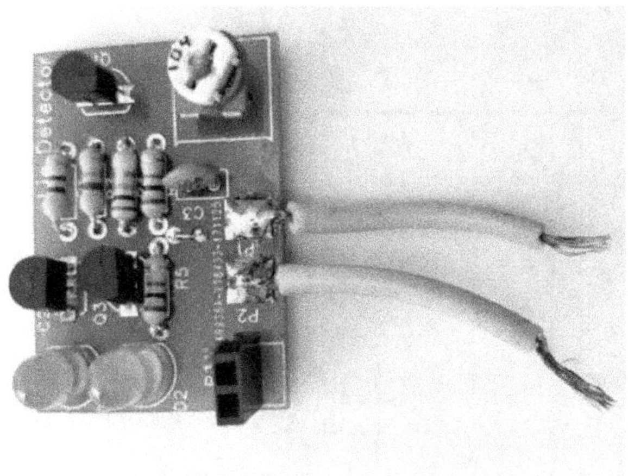

Working idea of Lie Detector Circuit:

The above circuit was reenacted in ISIS Proteus to check in the event that it functions true to form. It is constantly prescribed to test your circuit with reproduction before really assembling them. In the recreation the resistor R6 is thought to be the obstruction of the finger. At the point when no finger is put the estimation of resistor is limitlessness. So mimic that condition I have recently referenced the incentive to be 99999K.

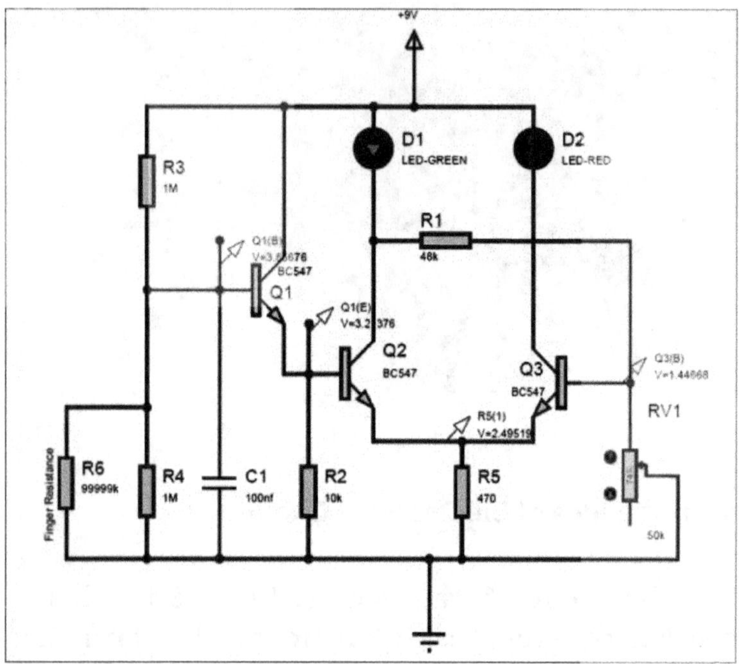

The green LED has turned on when no finger is put on the grounds that, the base voltage of Q1 and Q2 is around 3.2 voltage and henceforth the transistor is on making the Green LED to shine. Simultaneously since the Transistor Q2 is turned on, the base voltage over the transistor Q3 drops to be around 1.4V which will keep the transistor Q3 in off and consequently the Red LED is killed.

Presently how about we accept we have set our finger over the resistor R4 and thus the estimation of R6 tumbles to 50 ohms. This will influence the estimation of resistor R4 and consequently the red Light

Emitting Diode sparkles as demonstrated as follows.

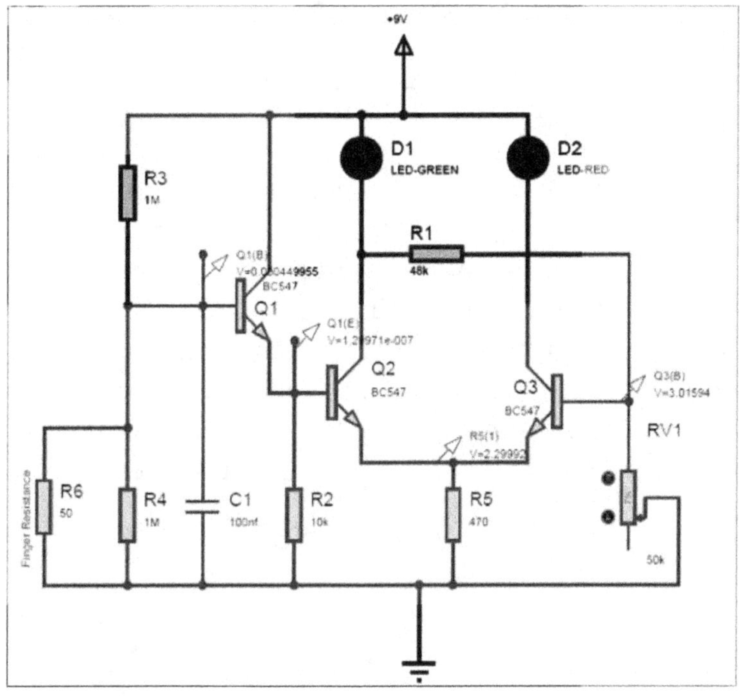

Presently the voltage drop across resistor R4 is less and consequently the base voltage of Transistor Q1 and Q2 is nearly 0V as appeared previously. This will keep them killed and in this way the Green LED won't shine. However, since the transistor Q2 is off the whole stock voltage gets separated between the resistor R1 and base of Q3. This makes the base voltage of Q3 to be 3V which is sufficient to turn it on. You can calibrate the base voltage more by utilizing the potentiometer too. On the off chance that the transistor Q3 is turned on the Red Light Emitting Diode will likewise shine as appeared previously.

Confirming the Circuit utilizing a breadboard:

As said before, we will manufacture a PCB for this Lie Detector Project. In case recreation fills in true to form it is constantly prescribed for apprentices to test the circuit utilizing a breadboard before really manufacturing a PCB. In this way you can ensure circuit fills in true to form and the parts are additionally accessible and working. My test circuit on breadboard looked something like this underneath

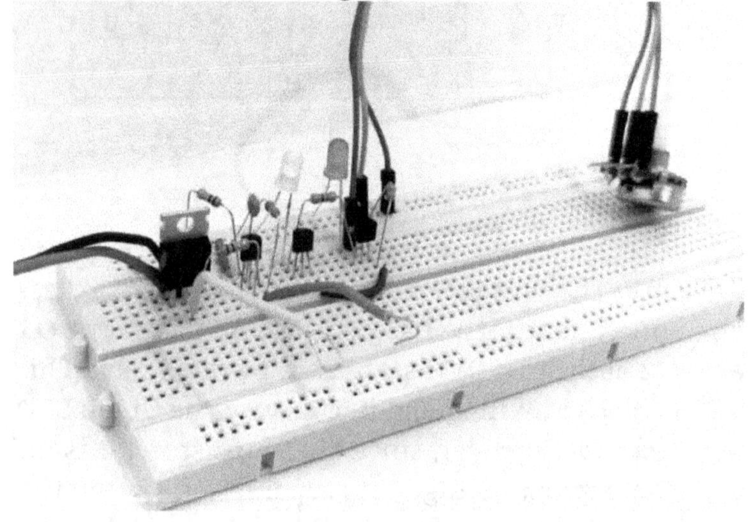

When you are happy with your Breadboard fabricate

it an opportunity to continue with PCB.

Circuit and PCB Design utilizing EasyEDA:

To structure this Lie locator Circuit, we have picked the online EDA device called EasyEDA. I have recently utilized EasyEDA commonly and thought that it was advantageous to use since it has a decent assortment of impressions and its open-source. Check here our all the PCB ventures. In the wake of structuring the PCB, we can arrange the PCB tests by their ease . They additionally offer part sourcing administration where they have an enormous load of electronic segments and clients can arrange their necessary segments alongside the PCB request.

While structuring your circuits and PCBs, you can likewise make your circuit and PCB plans open so different clients can duplicate or alter them and can take profit by there, we have additionally made our entire Circuit and PCB designs open for this Lie indicator circuit,
?

You can view any Layer (Top, Bottom, Topsilk, bottomsilk and so forth) of the Printed Circuit Board by choosing the layer structure the 'Layers' Window.

You can likewise see the PCB, how it will take care of creation utilizing the Photo View button in EasyEDA:

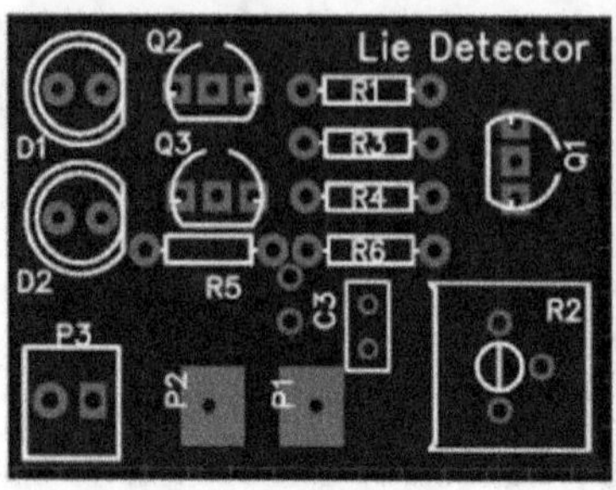

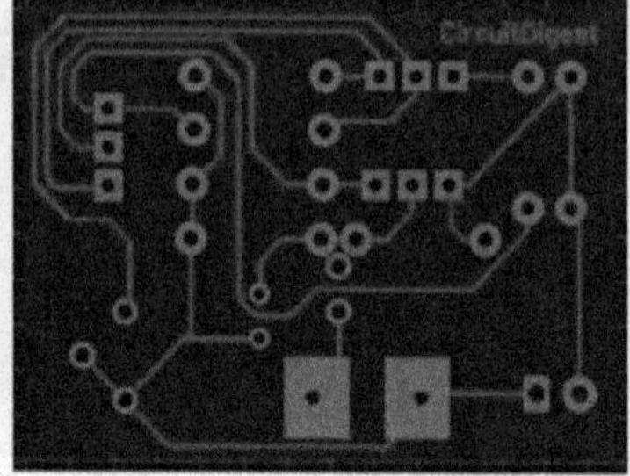

Ascertaining and Ordering Samples on the web:

Subsequent to finishing the structure of this Lie Detector PCB, you can arrange the PCB through . To arrange the PCB from JLCPCB, you need Gerber File. To download Gerber records of your PCB simply click the Fabrication Output button in EasyEDA editorial manager page, at that point download from the EasyEDA PCB request page.

Presently go to and click on Quote Now or Buy Now button, at that point you can choose the quantity of PCBs you need to arrange, what number of copper layers you need, the PCB thickness, copper weight, and even the PCB shading, similar to the depiction demonstrated as follows:

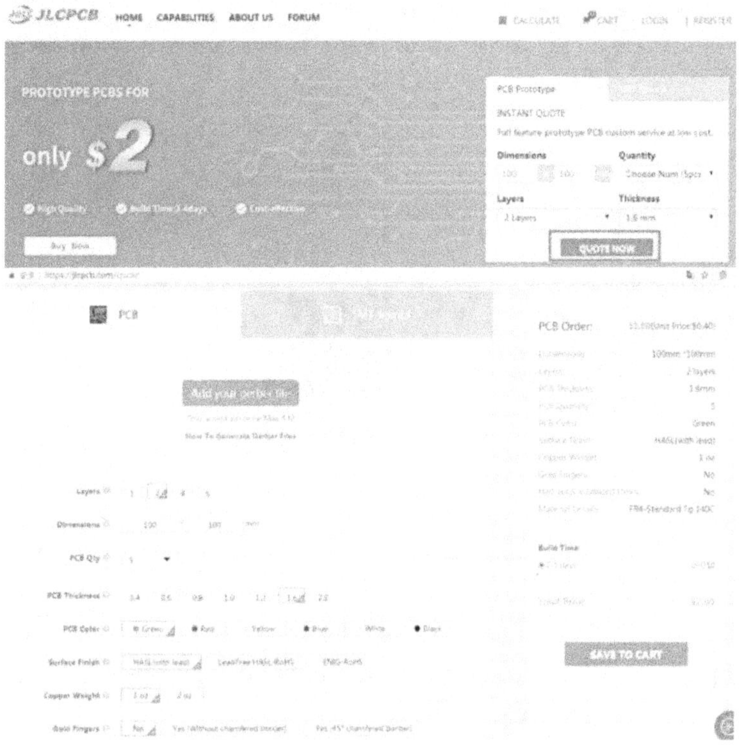

After you have chosen the entirety of the choices, click "Spare to Cart" and afterward you will be taken to the page where you can transfer your Gerber File which we have downloaded from EasyEDA. Transfer your Gerber document and snap "Spare to Cart". Lastly click on Checkout Securely to finish your request, at that point you will get your PCBs a 2 days after the fact. They are manufacturing the Printed Circuit Board at extremely low rate which is $2. Their construct time is likewise exceptionally less which is 48 hours with DHL conveyance of 3-5 days, fundamentally you will get your PCBs inside seven days of requesting.

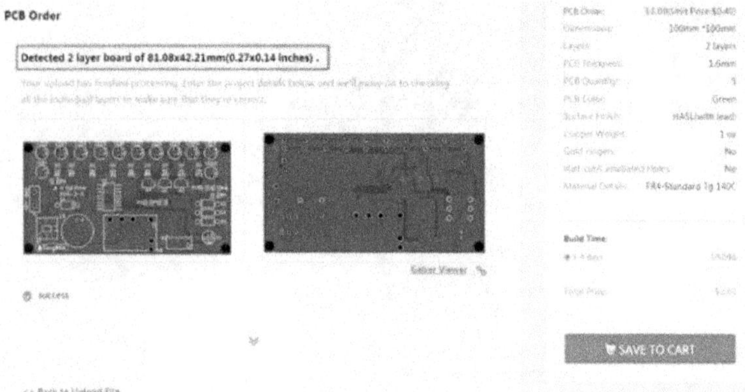

Following hardly any long periods of requesting PCB's I got the PCB tests in decent bundling as appeared in beneath pictures.

Also, in case of getting these pieces I have bound all the necessary parts over the PCB and connected a 9v Battery to it.

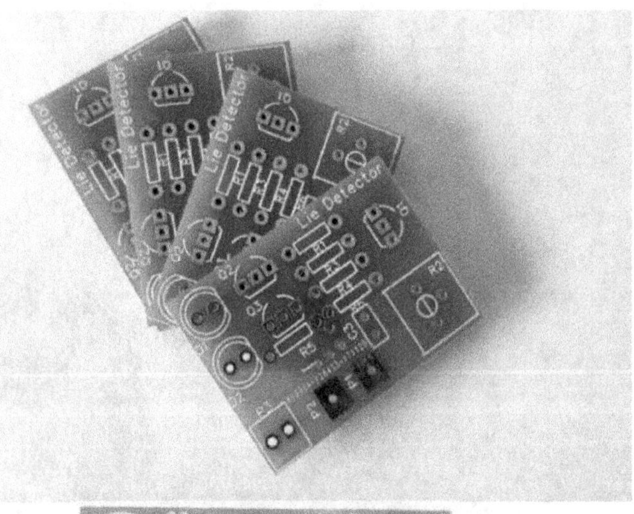

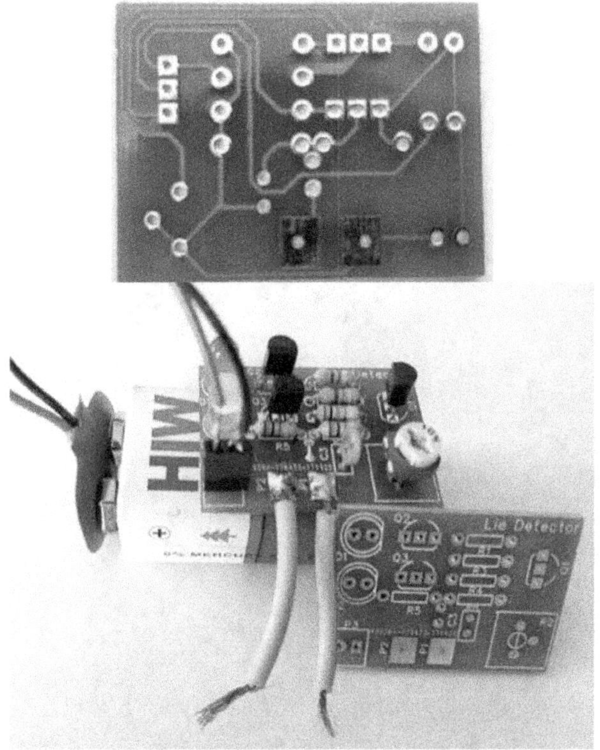

Falsehood Detector Circuit in real life:

When you have collected your load up it's an ideal opportunity to have a great time. Simply power it on with a nine V battery and you should see the green LED going high. In the event that you short the 2 yellow wires the green LED should turn on and the red should turn on. In the event that in this way, at that point it implies everything is filling in true to form. Presently ensure there is a touch of dampness on your hand and spot your finger on the wires, this should make the green LED to turn on and the red to kill. On the off chance that not, at that point, modify the potentiometer till the LED turns red.

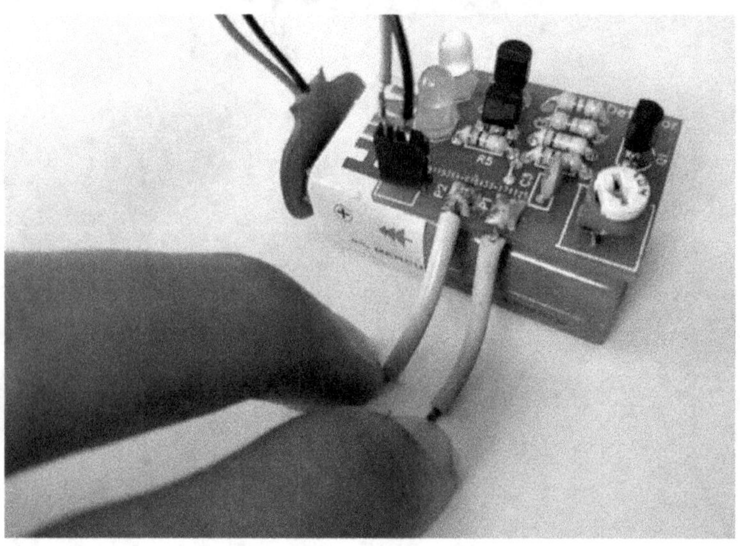

Presently, that the circuit is adjusted and is prepared for some trick. Since we have utilized a PCB the undertaking is profoundly compact and subsequently you can take it to your companions and have some good times time utilizing this. Expectation you got the venture working and took in something from this.

THANK YOU